The Hotel Years

Joseph Roth

Edited, translated and introduced
by Michael Hofmann

GRANTA

Granta Publications, 12 Addison Avenue, London W11 4QR

First published in Great Britain by Granta Books, 2015
This paperback edition published by Granta Books, 2016

Selection, translation and introduction
copyright © Michael Hofmann, 2015

Map copyright © Emily Faccini, 2015

The estate of Joseph Roth has asserted his moral right
under the Copyright, Designs and Patents Act, 1988,
to be identified as the author of this work.

Michael Hofmann has asserted his moral right under
the Copyright, Designs and Patents Act, 1988, to be
identified as the translator of this work.

The translation of this book was supported by
the Austrian federal chancellery.

A CIP catalogue record for this book is available
from the British Library.

1 3 5 7 9 10 8 6 4 2

ISBN 978 1 78378 128 7 (paperback)
ISBN 978 1 78378 129 4 (ebook)

Typeset by M Rules
Printed and bound by CPI Group (UK) Ltd, Croydon, CR0 4YY

JOSEPH ROTH (1894–1939) was the great elegist of the cosmopolitan, tolerant and doomed Central European culture that flourished in the dying days of the Austro-Hungarian Empire. Born into a Jewish family in Galicia, on the eastern edge of the empire, he was a prolific political journalist and novelist. On Hitler's assumption of power, he was obliged to leave Germany for Paris, where he died in poverty a few years later. His books include *What I Saw, Job, The White Cities, The String of Pearls, The Emperor's Tomb* and *The Radetzky March*, all published by Granta Books.

MICHAEL HOFMANN is the highly acclaimed translator of Hans Fallada, Wolfgang Koeppen, Kafka and Brecht, and the author of several books of poems and two books of criticism. He has translated thirteen previous titles by Joseph Roth. He teaches at the University of Florida in Gainesville.

'[Roth's] style is quick, dashed with colour and rendered vivid in English by Michael Hofmann ... In an explicit labour of love, the distinguished translator draws his favourite bits of Rothania into a multi-hued fresco of a raucous time and place ... A new classic'

Jewish Chronicle

'As good as any book in the series [of Hofmann's translations] and, at certain unheralded moments, better'   James Buchan, *Oldie*

'Atmospheric ... dark and funny'   *National Geographic Traveller*

'Dazzling ... An exquisite time capsule'   *Monocle*

'Poet Michael Hofmann most brilliantly conveys the fury that makes Roth special'   *Irish Times*

'Another wonderful volume of his beautifully observed journalism from the remains of the Habsburg Empire and beyond, and superbly translated (as ever) by Michael Hofmann'   *Times Higher Education*

'Roth is an indispensable writer and *The Hotel Years* is the indispensable introduc— ... ut so often startling ...   *...iew of Books*

Also by Joseph Roth

NON-FICTION

The White Cities: Reports from France, 1925–1939
(published in the United States as Report from a Parisian Paradise:
Essays from France, 1925–1939)
The Wandering Jews
What I Saw: Reports from Berlin, 1920–1933
Joseph Roth: A Life in Letters

FICTION

The Emperor's Tomb
The Collected Shorter Fiction of Joseph Roth
Rebellion
The String of Pearls
(published in the United States as The Tale of the 1002nd Night)
Right and Left
The Legend of the Holy Drinker
Job: The Story of a Simple Man
Confession of a Murderer
The Radetzky March
Flight Without End
The Silent Prophet
Hotel Savoy
Tarabas
The Antichrist
Weights and Measures
Zipper and His Father
The Spider's Web
The Leviathan
The Hundred Days

Contents

Part VII Pleasures and Pains

Part VIII Ending

Coda

EUROPE BETWEEN THE WARS

Introduction

Klaus Westermann's 1990 Kiepenheuer & Witsch edition of the complete works of Joseph Roth fills six blue-linen thin-paper volumes, each upward of a thousand pages. Three of these volumes are of fiction—from "Barbara", *The Spider's Web*, *Hotel Savoy*, and so on, to *Job* and *The Radetzky March*, through to the posthumously published *Legend of the Holy Drinker* and *The Leviathan*: just over a dozen novels and fragments, slightly more stories and novellas—and three are of non-fiction. In the course of his short life, Roth wrote many hundreds of newspaper articles. If Chekhov's wife was medicine, his was journalism—journalism in an unusually sweet and liberated and luxurious sense of the word, the wife in a hammock, with an umbrella drink, painting her toenails. "Rainbow-coloured soap bubbles" he called his pieces—when he wasn't getting on his high horse to his bosses, and telling them he was "sketching the portrait of an age". Over long periods, there are three, or four, or five articles a week, for the *Frankfurter Zeitung* and others. Roth was equal parts novelist and journalist. He wrote himself a perfect dumbbell. He can't have intended it, wouldn't even have known it (readers of his letters will recall that he lived out of two or three suitcases, and had no books, least of all his own), but the balance and parity in his work are exquisite and speaking. In a career spanning technically twenty-four, more realistically twenty years (from his return from the War in 1919 to his early death from alcoholism on 27 May 1939 at the age of forty-four) he therefore wrote between 250 and 300 published pages a year, not far short of one a day. Which in turn reminds me of something Joseph Brodsky used to say to me, long before I had begun to translate Roth at all (which happened in that same 1990): that there is a poem on every page of Roth's. Brodsky further liked the connection—if it is one; I think it is—between his surname and Roth's birthplace, Brody.

I HAVE TRANSLATED three books of Roth's non-fiction: *What I Saw* (which first introduced English readers to the word *feuilleton*— the little leaf or sheet, that practice of "saying true things on half a page" that was Roth's own definition of what he did) about Berlin; *The White Cities* (in the USA *Report from a Parisian Paradise*) about the South of France; and *The Wandering Jews* about the condition and perspectives of the various communities of Jews across Europe from East to West in the 1920s and '30s. *The Hotel Years* is the fourth, and my fourteenth of Roth altogether, and perhaps my last (though there always seems to be something else to do, or re-do, and I'm not at all sure I can contemplate life without him). As the title is supposed to intimate—because in fact all the years of Roth's maturity, after 1919, after university and army, were "hotel years"— it is nothing less than a new selection from everything and first principles (and no item here has been published in any of the other three books). It involved repeatedly going through the three blue non-fiction volumes and seeing what stuck, what went with what, what lived, what moved. There is no duty, no mission, no set sub- ject, no period, no place; I could please myself. Just as Roth went from hotel to hotel, and just as his pieces seem always to fly under his own flag and no other—one imagines, and he encourages one to imagine, in "A Man Reads the Paper", those pieces flanking his being written, so to speak, "in newspaper", while his are always written "in Roth"—so I went from article to article, choosing by turns something topical, something lasting, something burning, something whimsical. In 1930, Roth put out his own collection of recent *feuilletons* called *Panoptikum*; coming across a list of its contents, I am pleased to relate that fourteen of its twenty-eight pieces are here (while another two have already appeared in *What I Saw* and *The White Cities*). I am happy to say I don't think I strayed too far from his sense of himself.

QUITE EARLY ON, I decided to top and tail the selection: give it an envoi, and some lingering, echoic conclusion. The last thing is in a way the first: Roth's earliest memory—so he claimed—the loss of his cradle. (Surely he began as he meant to go on: in a letter of October 1932 he wrote, "The most powerful experience of my life was the war and the end of my fatherland, the only one I have ever had: the Dual Monarchy of Austria-Hungary." The cradle surely is a proleptic, poetic and darkly funny version of that later loss: one can imagine other auto-mythologists like Dylan Thomas coming up with something similar.) For a time I had three sections— Home, Away, and Hotels—which became five, and then eight. Fibonacci. Sixty-four pieces—eight squared. I ordered them as I might a book of poems. The order was to be basically chronological, but not rigidly so. I found sequences that I wanted—the celebrated hotel series, from 1929, evidently, but also the tours of Russia and Albania, and some of the domestic pieces from the Ruhrgebiet and elsewhere. I liked the idea of little out-of-place hostages (the bubble of Yin in the Yang) in some of the sections: a hotel piece, the "Hotel Kopriva", not in the hotel section; beginning the German section with something seen in Vienna; keeping a musical memory of the Volksgarten outside the Austria section, and a Russian piece ("The Opened Tomb") outside that devoted to the USSR. To name just a few. Any order so long as it's not too rigid. Half a dozen translations I ended up leaving out—the pieces weren't bad, the translations were OK, there was just no good place for them. They would have weakened the whole. Coverage was an aim; geography, evidently, but also history: the Great War and its aftermath; the Inflation, reparations and partial French occupation; the constant unrest and instability in Weimar Germany; politics, crime, style; emigration and exile; Communism, Fascism and Hitlerism. I collected a plurality of pieces on such archetypally Rothian themes as train travel, spring (which surely is his season, nor has anyone written better about it), oil-wells, interior design and balconies. And there are singular pieces on two gypsy girls met on the street, on a German-speaking blond Negro Frenchman, on a musical clown, a near-matricide, a morphine murderess. A trio of pieces on Roth's avatar and idol Heinrich Heine (another divided nature: German and Jew, poet and journalist, wit and agonist), the Austrian playwright Grillparzer, and a little known poet Eduard Samhaber represent Roth's taste and interest in literature. "Furlough in Jablonovka" (published posthumously in September 1939, with the Second World War under way) takes one back to before the first piece about men and dogs: to 1914 and World War One. In other words, the form is an unending spiral.

IT IS MY HOPE that these pieces will take the English reader closer to Roth than anything else he wrote. For once, there is no story, no dependable subject, no histrionics (as often in the letters, in an inextricable and worsening situation). He comes into these pieces as nowhere else: it is him walking the gypsy girls over the road; loosely impersonating a millionaire; making landfall in Albania (in that exquisite piece); checking in and out of his hotel "fatherland"; taking the tram ride from nowhere to nowhere, but getting a little closer all the time to the end of the world, in the Ruhr. It is his mind, his graceful spirit, his leaps and flights, his noticings that he parlays into pieces here. His supplying and withholding of contexts; his exaggerations and his subtlety; his irony, his humanity and his blank hatreds (say, of the nationalist duelling fraternity students). His modesty and his nettled arrogance ("Interviews are an alibi for a journalist's lack of ideas"). His sublime gift for phrases ("Saint Petroleum"); the asperity and reasonableness of his conclusions ("That's what is missing in Germany: the regulating consciousness"); his gorgeous tirades—

> The colour of the age is white, laboratory white, as white as the room where they invented lewisite, white as a church, white as a bathroom, white as a dissecting room, white as steel and white as chalk, white as hygiene, white as a butcher's apron, white as an operating table, white as death, and white as the age's fear of death! Let's brighten up the ceiling! — Because it is the age's belief that white is cheerful. It wants by brightness to attract cheerful people. And the people are as merry as patients, and the present is as merry as a hospital.

—and his feline way with form: "The Wonders of Astrakhan" works like an auction: first the fish have it, then the flies, then, with a surprising late bid, the beggars. It is with his variable thoughts on exile, on monarchy, on literature, on the military, on nations, on East and West, that he regales us. He is capable of hanging a set of political opinions on a quirk of facial hair styling ("a large blond moustache that went out into a couple of butchers' hooks") and of turning a manicure into a threat ("a hand with flashing pink nails dangled over the chairback"); of inferring the state of the nation from a chance observation (the railway conductor wolfing chocolates), and of shrinking another nation into a natty synecdoche ("on the right a mosque, on the left a rudimentary café terrace where guests bake and fezzes talk"). He has at times a wonderfully simple, radical imagination: Grillparzer's visit to Goethe (one of the great humiliations in literary history, and not the only one involving

Goethe) is like Friday visiting Sunday, "and then going home, satisfied and sad that he was Friday"; the scene at Boryslav—the primitive oil-wells—makes him think of capitalism lurching into expressionism. A hotel can be either a canny form of post-national organization, taking its inspiration from the sadly defunct Dual Monarchy ("He is an Italian. The waiter is from Upper Austria. The porter is a Frenchman from Provence. The receptionist is from Normandy. The head waiter is Bavarian. The chambermaid is Swiss. The valet is Dutch. The manager is Levantine; and for years I've suspected the cook of being Czech"), or sometimes just a motiveless and fantastic gyre:

> The "Hotel Kopriva" is always between trains. Its eighty rooms and hundred and twenty beds whirl round and round. The "Hotel Kopriva" doesn't exist. It merely seems to exist. The gramophone tumbles upstairs and down. The sample cases fly through the air. The manager rushes from room to room. The room-service waiter runs to the train. The porter is knocked for six. The manager is the room-service waiter. The porter is the manager. The room-service waiter is the porter. The room numbers are departure times. The clock is a timetable. The visitors are tied to the station on invisible elastics. They bounce back and forth. The gramophone sings train sounds. Eighty makes a hundred and twenty. A hundred and twenty rooms trundle through eighty beds.

Roth may indeed have sketched the portrait of his age, but these pieces also make a portrait of their author: wilful and versatile, aggressive and benign, beautiful and drawn to ugliness, everywhere and nowhere (Tirana and Baku and the railway junction at 4 a.m.), philanthropical and misanthropical, endlessly spooked and endlessly observant. Surely among other more-or-less intended self-portraits (the grave Grillparzer the obvious example) he is also

Grock, the musical clown, the multi-instrumentalist in a world of "exemplary mediocrity", who plays everything, even his balled-up gloves, and is finally incapable by himself of finding his way off-stage:

a sad face full of noble ugliness, an aristocrat in a crude world, a man of noble truth betrayed a thousand times, an honest, yes, a humble striver who always comes a cropper, a man born for despair who forces himself to believe, a clumsy so-and-so, a hero, a lofty man in the depths, defeated a thousand times but always victorious.

Michael Hofmann
Gainesville, Florida
February 2015

Envoi

A Man Reads the Paper

(1926)

The expression on the face of the newspaper reader is serious, sometimes tending to grim, occasionally dissolving in smiling hilarity. While his slightly bulbous pupils in their sharp oval spectacles slalom down the page, dreamy fingers play on the café table and perform a silent trill that looks like a form of grief—as though the fingertips were feeling for invisible crumbs to pick up.

The newspaper reader has a long, well-trimmed shovel beard that covers the feuilleton page while he attends to the political news. Half-obscured by the beard, in sumptuous purple splendour, shimmers a bow tie whose knot I am unable to see, except when the newspaper reader thoughtfully strokes his Adam's apple.

I can see what is engaging the newspaper reader's attention: the recent sensational reports from Budapest. They have been given a bold headline. They are presented in a fluffy, tempting, positively beguiling layout, in numerous little paragraphs, each one of which has its own alluring subtitle. Like all news, they give themselves away before they can be transmitted: and they give away more than they can possibly keep.

It is impossible to see them as anything but sensationalist. They are about the passing of false bills, but they don't tell the whole story. They are scrupulously accurate and yet still they withhold a few details. They describe the character of the counterfeiter, but they don't know his name. They refer to "well-placed sources", but where and how they are placed they don't say. Of course, it's the things you're not told that arouse your interest. The gaps in the news are the interesting bits.

So what happens now in the newspaper reader? How will he react to what he has not read? Is he pleased to learn about the false bills, or upset, or is he even from Budapest himself? Surely he may be numbered among the great horde of the morally indignant, who feel vicarious anger at any news of criminality. All the fuses that were slowly burning in him reach the point at which they cause an explosion. Not visibly, of course. Heavens, no! But one that is contained in itself, more an implosion ...

In any case, it may be seen that the reports are toying with his delicate soul, even while he imagines he is toying with the news. If he weren't so utterly bespectacled, it might almost be that the news is reading him. Perhaps he imagines his mind is toying with these half-reported things, filling them out. But these special reports take it out of him. A leader's shallow scoop would do him in. Everything there is so agleam with shiny common sense that the reader can't but be dazzled.

Now he stands up, the reader, fully in the picture, older, wiser and possibly sadder. With his left hand he smoothes away any unevennesses that may have occurred in his beard and changes his glasses. (For an instant he has shy little mousy eyes.) Then he snaps open a coffin containing a different pair, and heads outside, equipped for the street.

The feuilleton remained covered. He leaves it to less manly natures than his own.

But if it should happen that one day, quietly, out of boredom, he should read it, then he would not like it one little bit. Because what I write is not to his taste ...

Frankfurter Zeitung, 11 January 1926

Part I

Germany

Of Dogs and Men
(1919)

To the many scenes of war misery in Vienna a new one was added, a few days ago.

A man returned from the war in the form of a hinge—invalid with shattered spine—moves almost inexplicably through Kärntner Strasse, selling newspapers. A dog sits on his back.

A clever, well-trained dog, riding on his own master, and making sure he doesn't lose a single paper. A modern fairy-tale being, combination of man and dog, thrown up by the war and set down in the misery of Kärntner Strasse.

A sign of the times, in which dogs ride men, to protect them from other men. A memory of those great times when men were trained like dogs and were barked at as "Schweinehunde" and so forth, by others who were themselves bloodhounds (though heaven help you if you called them that).

An outcome of patriotism that makes the upright likenesses of the Creator dependent on four-footed creatures who lacked the spiritual distinction to become heroes or cannon-fodder, and at the most did odd jobs in the ambulance service. On the invalid's chest dangles an Emperor Karl Troop Cross. On the neck of the dog a mere dog-tag.

The bearer of the Troop Cross is a victim. The one with the dog-tag is active. He guards the suffering of the invalid. He keeps the man from further harm. His Fatherland and fellow-beings could only hurt him. He has them to thank for being watched over by a dog. Sign of the times! Once there were sheepdogs who watched herds of sheep, and guard-dogs that guarded houses. Today there are mandogs who watch invalids, mandogs the logical consequence of submissive men. The scene struck me with the force of a revelation: a dog seated on a man. When he remembers what happened when he relied on other men, a man is happy to put his trust in a dog. Is there anything so sad as this sight, which seems so emblematic? All around stroll the war-profiteers with their X-ray vision, and in the midst of everything a mounted dog. The human race has lost, all hail to the animal. We have been through the war that was the last hurrah of cavalry, and at the end of it dogs ride around on men.

Der Neue Tag, 1 August 1919

3

Millionaire for an Hour
(1921)

Every so often, I like to spend a little time in the lobby of the big hotel where visitors from hard-currency nations come to stay. The coffered ceiling consists of so many gorgeous panels, and in the middle of each one sprouts an electric light. The lamps look like glass flowers, shaded by golden leaves.

The ceiling is low but expansive, the furniture likewise. Everything here tends to breadth and luxury. The low ceiling murmurs: Don't get up! The broad armchairs say: Kick your shoes off!

I kick off one of my shoes and look with a deal of satisfaction at the crease of my trouser leg (my only pair, but let that go). I also take pride in the state of my toe caps, which have just had a good shine from the soft flannel cloth of the man on Unter den Linden.

After just a quarter of an hour of sitting like that, and feeling flush and expansive, I start to think I am someone from a hard-currency country, and am staying at the hotel.

The messenger boy who is delivering a letter gives my shiny toecaps a wide berth. The messenger boy has no idea I don't live here. When I call him, he comes to a stop outside the charmed hard-currency nimbus in whose centre I am sitting, and doffs his brown cap to me with an angular movement of his well-trained arm. He has big blue eyes and gives me his best awestruck stare. He has whole magazines of respect in his eyes. He is apple-cheeked

and smells pleasantly of milk, like a clean baby. He has been study-
ing deference to his hard-currency elders for all of two years now.

The white napkin of the waiter starts to twitch respectfully at
about ten paces. The hotel manager, striding across the tasteful
ornaments of his Smyrna carpet with the dignity of a Grand Vizier,
inclines his head when I look at him.

After a while, I shift my focus to my brother millionaires. They
are very well dressed. The men smell of new leather luggage and
English shaving cream and coal. The women disperse gentle hints
of a Russian scent across the room. The bittersweet aroma tickles
my nostrils, only to disappear again.

The millionaires are gifted poseurs. The younger ones wear
belted lemon-lime raincoats with discreet matte buckles. Their hats
are for the most part dove-grey and have a hint of a dent at the top
(that might almost be an accident). Their gloves are white, their
shoes are brown or tan, and when the young millionaires sit down,
they give their trousers a little tweak at the knees to show off their
silk socks.

The old millionaires seem generally unaware of the season. It's
not the state of the mercury but the state of the market that matters. The old millionaires sit there in their winter wool coats and
padded gloves, and they keep a freshly guillotined cigar clenched
so expectantly between their teeth that a waiter leaps by with tails
aflutter, in mid-air striking a match on the emery board so as to
have it ready when he alights.

I get to know people here: a man with whiskers who looks like
a Hamburg senator (and he has the thick 's' to match). Protracted
negotiations with a belted youth. The subject is petroleum. The
youth seems to be from Poland. He has a piece of paper in his top
pocket. Every so often he gives it a meaningful tap. Each time the
bewhiskered oldster falls silent and looks wistfully at the youth.

Behind a column, a mulatto leans back in a rattan chair. He is
smoking a dense Turkish cigarette and is negotiating with a spiv of

an uncertain age who fancies himself a matinee idol. He has a pair of canary-yellow gloves. You can practically hear them cheeping away. He is wearing the right one, the left is lying casually and emptily on the marble table top. Abruptly the spiv bestirs himself, gets to his feet, and gives the mulatto a friendly wave with his empty glove, as though his train were just pulling out. It's my sense that he's got one over on the mulatto. Men in canary-yellow gloves should be treated with suspicion.

In the lobby cocaine, sugar, political systems, revolutions and women are on offer. A Russian count ponders the advisability of a move for the naval base of Kronstadt. A carpet dealer discusses terms with an only recently "made" man. A lawyer takes receipt of half a dozen passports from a Russian family. "We'll get it done," his eyes seem to blink. He jabs his pince-nez against the bridge of his nose, and with sudden resolve clacks his briefcase shut. As he reverses out of the door he bows three times to the Russian head of household, who waves avuncularly.

At five the band launch into the Peer Gynt Suite. The millionaires turn away from their business and towards their womenfolk. The millionairesses drink mocha and eat ice cream and nibble little cakes and make sure their right pinkie is always extended, as though it were an especially holy thing that mustn't ever touch the side of a cup.

When I leave the hotel the porter stands beside the revolving door, primed to greet me, like a talking fork. His owner's monogram decorates him heart and head. A chauffeur asks me whether I would like a ride somewhere.

I would not. I am no longer a millionaire.

Neue Berliner Zeitung—12 Uhr-Blatt, 1 April 1921

4

The Umbrella
(1921)

It was raining the day before yesterday. The asphalt of the Kurfürstendamm was slippery, and a woman with an open umbrella ran into a moving car, slipped, and was run over. Her umbrella was lying on the pavement. People rushed over, the woman was picked up; she was badly shaken, nothing more—all this had to be established in a nearby café. But before it could be established, and while she was still lying in the road, covered with blood in the imagination of all the passers-by who had witnessed the accident, and possibly with severed limbs, a man had the presence of mind to pick up the lady's umbrella and walk off with it.

I had never supposed that people's decency was a match for their self-interest. But that their meanness was even greater than their curiosity, that was brought home to me by this incident, which shows that it isn't difficult to strip the pillow off someone's deathbed, and sell the feathers at the next street corner.

The woman who had escaped with her life now wept for the loss of her umbrella and was not at all grateful that her limbs were intact. As evidenced here, people come in two sorts: unscrupulous and plain dim.

Neue Berliner Zeitung—12 Uhr-Blatt, 29 May 1921

5

The Emigrants' Ship
(1923)

On board the Pittsburgh

The emigrants' ship is called the *Pittsburgh*, and it is due to leave Bremerhaven at exactly 2 minutes past 11. The emigrants are people from the East, mainly Jews, lucky to have escaped the Europe of pogroms; also Russian peasants and young Ukrainian women, with colourful headscarves like summer meadows, sprinkled with cheery red and blue flowers. The White Star Line, which owns the *Pittsburgh*, has finally ended its rather anachronistic policy of "steerage passengers", by abolishing the 'tween decks, and introducing third-class cabins. The proletarian romance of a chaos of people and suitcases is over. All are tucked away in tight cabins like lockable pigeonholes set in the walls. The Jews, children or bearded, the Russian peasants, their faces furrowed like their fields, and the shining Ukrainian peasant women are all boxed up. Their emigrant poverty hidden, no longer open to the shameless prying eye. Still, there is a good deal of misery on show before it is all packed away. The luggage—strange, eccentric-looking items, down pillows bagged up in hessian, coverlets, red and white striped privities, tied and endlessly retied bundles and baskets with antediluvian padlocks. Everything is loaded onto small wagons running on electric motors and taken to port. Even so, the emigrants are still carrying a lot. There are things a person doesn't like to lose from sight, not even for half an hour. And so the Jews are left to sweat under their cherished loads which they lug on their crooked backs and in their frozen hands as far as the plump, helmeted policeman. This policeman is a splendid instance of a half-terrestrial, half-marine authority. His round cheeks are of a red that seems to glow from within, as if he had a lit candle in his mouth like a paper lantern at a summer fete. Ships' cooks all look like that. The helmet, the dark cloak, and the sabre, none of them go with the salt water face. A great calm radiates from that broad, improbably luminous face, and a benevolence that denies the severity of the blinking badge on the helmet, and quite disavows the sabre. The policeman stands at the far end of the narrow bridge that connects terra firma to the great sea. The emigrants need to go past him with their heavy loads. Clumsily as can be, they set their loads down, looking for a clean spot; ideally they would spread one of their red and blue check handkerchiefs on the ground before setting their bundle down on top of it. All that takes a good five minutes, and already a gong is being sounded on board: in ten minutes the *Washington* is due, and so the *Pittsburgh* will have to leave its berth. But the policeman radiates the calm and ease of a traffic light; they look at him, and think they have all the time in the world, whatever the urgency of the ship. They produce passports and tickets sewn into undershirts or variously secreted about their bodies. The policeman, by the light of his own countenance, studies them assiduously.

The ship (it has a tonnage of 16,000) carries 1,800 passengers. About a third of these are emigrants. They come from Russia and the Successor states, Poland and Lithuania. The East of Europe pours them out. These Eastern Jews and peasants have been emigrating westwards for hundreds of years, leaving their old homes behind, looking for a new one. A great sadness emanates from

them, their grey beards, their wrinkled faces, their adorable, helpless bundles. A family from Kowel is here, an old matron swaddled
in black, two young daughters with cropped curls, and a twenty-
year-old son, with broad shoulders and red hands dangling from his
sleeves like giant appliances. He laughs and shrugs his strong
shoulders. For two years now he and his family have been wandering through the sorry, moribund West of Europe, in search of
his father, who left Kovel ten years before—God only knows where
he is. They were in Budapest, six months in constant dread of the
expatriation that might come at any hour of day or night; finally it
came and they were chased to Vienna, where they hung on for a
year in a basement hole on Kleine Schiffergasse. Here too they
were viewed as a burden on the state—the son engaged in unau-
thorized selling of clothes—and they drifted on to the wretched
east of Berlin, to Hirtenstrasse, where the black market promises
undreamed-of riches and doesn't deliver. Finally a cousin got in
touch from New York, a street vendor of oranges and lemons and
he sent them steamer tickets and ten dollars apiece—God helps
those who are abandoned. Now they are on their way to America
and a vast, beautiful freedom beckons to the children, a grave to
their old mother, but they will have got away from Europe, the
continent of pogroms, of the police, the black market and unau-
thorized dealing in second-hand clothes. The Ukrainian peasants
are fleeing hunger, the plague, and a creeping charity. One has a
brother-in-law there—Nikita is his name—another has a nephew,
Timofei. The barely legible addresses are scribbled on old crum-
pled envelopes. For many weeks the peasants have been carrying
them tucked into waistcoat pockets, in snuff boxes, and in carved
pipe bowls of cherry wood. The peasants' wives have the timid,
flickering eyes of frightened animals as they watch the bustle, great
ships' cranes taking up huge quantities of coals, slowly swivelling
in mid-air, the scoops opening like giant hands, and spilling their
load into the hold. They hear the unfamiliar clang of the heavy

ship's bell, the warning cries of the dockers, the thunder or clatter of the rolling trucks. They see how the harbour goes on and on, offering the illimitable ocean to the eye, a never-before-seen endlessness of blue.

Way up in the air the Stars and Stripes flutter over the international shipping banner, which is as blue as the sky and the sea, and with a white circle in the middle, like a perfectly regular cloud. On the bridge stands a man with his cap strapped over chin and ears, giving out orders in incomprehensible terms. His commands are as mysterious as the great sea itself. A little tug tows the ship with thick hawsers; like a willing triumphal gate the harbour locks slowly and ceremonially open. The emigrants are on board; they call out to the disappearing land. No one has come to see them off, so they wave to strangers, to the luminous policeman, to the dockers and porters. Up at the rim of a huge chimney appears a black figure, a chimneysweep, a toy figure compared to the enormous liner, so tiny is his silhouette against the endless blue background. Out of the perfectly round windows of their cabins the emigrants' faces catch their last sight of Europe.

Prager Tagblatt, 18 February 1923

The Currency-Reformed City
(1924)

The only affordable currency-reformed city in Germany is Hamburg. It has introduced its own currency, the much-praised, much-sought-after Hamburg Gold Mark, which sells at a premium on the black market. I have seen one for myself, a Hamburg Gold Mark, it's a little scrap of paper that proclaims that the Hamburg banks will vouch for its full convertibility. And as people know the world over, Hamburg banks are solid and reliable, and so Hamburg has become the cheapest, most affordable city in Germany.

A hotel room costs half a dollar, lunch costs a quarter of a dollar, a taxi ride costs half a dollar, a pound of meat costs a dollar. There is unemployment. Unemployed dockworkers, laid-off sailors and factory workers. A month ago there was a risk that this great mass of unemployed, cultivated assiduously by communist and national-ist propaganda, might spark a revolution, or at the very least a series of disturbances. And lo! The Hamburg Gold Mark came along, and everything went quiet. It's one of the mysteries of economics why a great mass of hungry people, none of whom have so much as a Hamburg gold pfennig to their name, are pacified by the existence of the Hamburg Gold Mark. Greybeard economists scratch their heads at this wonder. Although no one knows how long it will last.

No one knows, because in waterside dives, in shady bars haunted by desperate people, sailors who have missed their ships, criminals hunted by the police forces of various cities and countries—in these sinister breeding-grounds of international crime, what has been on the agenda for the last few months is politics. A curious kind of politics. People who were left cold by the European economy or the constitutional arrangements of the German Reich, for whom swastika and red star are emblems of foreign worlds, not for outsiders, for people outside of society, these same people now spend all their evenings in smoke-filled rooms—not because they're interested in the speeches, but because they are given food there, and schnapps and—money. The Hamburg Gold Mark, as they say, rolls almost as well as the Soviet rouble, and a lot better than the old Czarist one. It appears that forces unknown are competing over the *lumpenproletariat* of port cities. Nowhere is the propaganda of left and right more virulent than in Hamburg and Bremen. Odd that these are two cities with a particularly conservative middle class. One might have supposed that looking out every day at so much water would have broadened their intellectual horizons and their sense of the political necessities of the fatherland. But it is in these places that social progress encounters the toughest resistance. The contradictions are unbridgeable. Nationalist propaganda appeals to the irate middle class, which one wouldn't have thought so absurdly susceptible. Communist propaganda is favoured by the stiff necks of the merely rich middle class. In no German city is there such fierce hatred of the poor. Nowhere is the obstinacy of the propertied classes stronger.

For the time being, the Hamburg Gold Mark has calmed people down. In the long run, though, no unemployed man can take comfort from the fact that his fellow in work can now afford to buy butter. Without the free food he gets in assembly halls he would starve to death. And in these assembly halls, where people used to go to smooch and drink, they are now daubing swastikas and Soviet stars on the grimy walls.

Prager Tagblatt, 6 January 1924

Baltic Tour
(1924)

The "season"—it's a technical term—has begun very auspiciously on the Baltic coast. Here too, as in watering places the world over, there is early, late and high season. High is just beginning now, in July, late won't start till the end of August. Both have so many subscribers already that most hotels, villas and B&Bs are booked up. This summer promises to be exceptionally profitable for the leisure industry and the local inhabitants of the Baltic beaches. They deserve it. The summer visitor, who only sees the sea and the coast by sunshine, or at worst, in wretched squalls lasting several days, has of course no notion of the difficulties faced by the locals in autumn, winter and early spring. The Baltic is not always as clement as it is during the "season". When tourists are a distant twinkle, the coast often plays host to a primal struggle between inhabitants and elements. What these not overly well-off little communities spend a deal of money and patience building, in the way of bridges, beach huts and little wooden towers, can quite easily be destroyed by a storm in the course of one spring night. The first and most important prerequisite for living here is a basic toughness. I have talked to locals, they have told me about the harsh, white, unending winters, winters in which no one goes out of doors, in which the snow buries the buildings, the electricity and gas don't work, water freezes in the wells, and the onshore gale blows with such merciless force that no living being can stand up to it. Summer means more to the residents than recovery, or getting well or resurrection. In the course of those cruel winters they have learned to be tight-lipped, tough, suspicious, stubborn. Even so, a generous humanity stirs in them, their hospitality is sincere, their expressions simple, their greetings curt but friendly. In our many-faceted, tribal Germany this is one of the most interesting populations. Their songs are as simple as the rhythm of the sea; their language is rich in foursquare consonants that resist the prevailing wind, to make themselves heard. One can't hold it against these people that they charge such relatively high prices, higher for the moment than in the South of France. The beauties of the Baltic coast are worth it. Further, the baths are closer than foreign resorts, and then—they are ours. We go there and do well for ourselves. A room and board costs between seven and ten marks per visitor per day. The early season is three marks less.

The Baltic sea baths have a greater array of natural beauties than most European spas. They are characterized by an almost improbable combination of rural variety and the eternal monotony of the sea. One can walk for days with the sea on one side, and a landscape of the most variable composition on the other. Hills, dales, woods and sea, sea, sea. One rises early and hears the surf beat on the shore, a swelling and ebbing crash. There is the kiss of the wave which combines coming and going, arrival and departure, greeting with the pain of separation—and at the same time there is the song of myriad wood-birds, an almost exotic choir, so that you would think yourself somewhere far in the south. You come here expecting only sea and screaming seagulls. But here is the melodious variety of a continental broad-leaved forest, opposing the water's monotony with dedication and energy. It's so unexpected to hear bird-twitter and surf-crash at once that you think you must be dreaming and it takes a while to gradually get used to the fairy-tale pairing of contrasting melodies.

The leading resorts, Swinemünde, Heringsdorf, Bansin, Ahlbeck, are well known; the island of Rügen less well. Most land-lubbers come over all awestruck at the idea of an island; places like that must be wildly inaccessible. And so, even though, or perhaps just because it's so self-evident, you say it again: the sea-bathing on Rügen is as comfortable, as European, and as civilized as anywhere on the European coast. They have electricity, gas, running water, telephone, hairdressers, baths, hotels. And they have more, too: namely that smidgeon of intact nature that serves to guarantee the civilized townie respite from civilization. You can get a shave, send a telegram, listen to the band, and yet still go on a solitary ramble through charmed scenery, and run into a fisherman who might have lurched from the pages of Grimm. In Binz, the largest of the Rügen resorts, it's difficult to avoid the jazz. Poetically inclined natures and canny admen have dubbed it "the Sorrento of the north". It has twenty hotels and two hundred villas to let, a two-mile seafront promenade, is stuffed with make-up, powder, atropine, tennis racquets and sharp pleats, cocktail bars and tipsy customers; a spa hotel with dancing opportunities for black tie and evening gowns; and even some swastika flags. In Sassnitz you can be one of 26,000 visitors, and still do something for your immortal soul, and visit an Evangelical and Catholic Mass. It lies in a dip, protected to the north by beech-clad hills, and not far, a two-hour walk, is Stubbenkammer. Here the sand and clay soil is relieved by chalk. This is the terrain of the old pirate legends. The chalk cliffs are extraordinary, at night they have a ghostly glow, they seem pre-destined for pirate tales. The chalk bluffs have faces and eerie formations, and there's a very strange contradiction between the deathly pallor of the material and its lively, grimacing forms.

If you're looking for quiet, national characteristics, idylls—you will look up the small resorts of Sellin, Baabe, Göhren, Thiessow, Putbus, or Lauterbach. Here the waiters wear less rigidly starched shirtfronts and the hosts speak Plattdeutsch. Hens peck about on the streets, and a beautiful woman may walk through the little town in a bathrobe. The village-like quiet is disturbed only by the occasional marching band. No jazz stirs the wrath of Neptune and his fellow sea-gods. And if you're in luck, you'll see some of the old Mönchgut residents dancing in their traditional costume. They wear homespun clothes, black robes, colourful waistcoats, golden chains and short, baggy white pantaloons, billowing round short rubber boots, looking like bells. Their legs are like thin clappers— even with the boots. They are the last of the dancers. The young farmers have given up weaving, and don't dance any more. A whole way of life is coming to an end.

Visitors eager to avoid politics* should seek out Baabe, which is one of the quietest and cheapest of the Baltic resorts and which is run by its clever, efficient and modern mayor, Thormann. But in other places too the locals have not had their heads turned by swastikas, and what there is by way of nationalist propaganda is imported by the visitors.

The sea, meanwhile, is as it always is, clean and untouched by the childish and violent games of men. You gaze at the infinity of water and sky, and forget. The wind that billows out the swastika banner does so in all innocence. The wave in which it is reflected isn't to blame for its own desecration. So foolish are people that even in sight of these eternal things, they do not shrink in awe.

Frankfurter Zeitung, 6 July 1924

---

* Politics: there is a late shadow cast over this enthusiastic piece by the phenomenon of "*Bäder-Antisemitismus*", the anti-semitism prevalent in some North German resorts from about 1890. Roth handles it discreetly and a little disdainfully, but it's very evidently there.

8

Melancholy of a Tram Car in the Ruhr

(1926)

A thin, persistent rain. The tram leaves at twelve-fifteen. At one-forty-five it will be in the next town. The stop is outside a bar. I sip kirsch, and peer out at the street through the ornaments in the net curtains. Rain like this stifles sounds as much as snow does. Yes, if these curtains had no ornaments, if this bar had no curtains—why curtains?—then I could probably have seen the tram approach. I shudder at the thought of it leaving without me, and at the same time I wish it would. Then I might take the quicker, more comfortable, reliable train instead. But I am under the spell of a freely chosen torment. The more time, patience, chill, kirsch and loathing I sink into this endeavour, the more difficult it is for me to give it up. Time flows, rain flows.

Quite punctually, no reason it should, the tram comes. Its running board is high and sodden; the floor on the inside is damp too. An old man is smoking a pipe, a woman sits with a covered basket on her lap, schoolgirls clamber aboard, with rough, ugly satchels on their backs that the rain has darkened—like soldiers' knapsacks with dangling sponge attached. Two workingmen lean on the back platform, keeping the conductor company. There is a country maid as well, with gold-rimmed spectacles and bare feet. She puts me in mind of a plough pulled by a locomotive. No one speaks. All are preparing themselves for the ordeal of a long ride. Such concentration demands complete silence. The hard seats of shiny polished wood are not only short; they also have a downward slope. Sitting on them means: continually and hopelessly shuffling back up.

We go along a long road with dark buildings and dark spaces between them; plots with boards and fences that make no sense, no hope of ever becoming a garden, a field, or a house. The dead bodies of plots. The town refuses to end. If it ever does, though, you can be sure the next one will begin immediately. The towns hand the streets on. Each time, we stop in front of brown shelters of creosoted wood that look like the primal forms of stations in the wilder parts of America. Next come allotments, little hutments of roofing cardboard, the summer castles of the little man and the little rabbit. Jugs, pots and bowls have been spiked on fence-posts like so many severed heads. A red-brick factory, an iron fence, a little white stone gate-house with a visible clock-punch, behind it big puffing chimneys, four, five, six of them, ready to reproduce at a moment's notice.

The country keeps being on the point of taking over, and making country again—and then it can't. There are no buildings. The road could turn into a country road at this point. There are even trees at either side, preparing to speak up for it. But our tram needs its overhead wires, and the wires need long, bare, wooden poles, with a couple of china pots flowering at the top end, for purposes of electricity. A caricature of a snowdrop.

In the far distance, on the very horizon, nature is at pains to produce a wood. But there is no wood. There is a kind of beginning vegetative bald patch with comb-over fronds of pine. Next come the inns, one after the other, and each one announcing "picturesque garden location". What can they mean, what is picturesque here? I imagine a restaurant with painted orange trees and laurel in flower pots; or a bit of a cabbage patch with a veranda; four fences festooned with wild Virginia creeper. There are no limits to the imagination.

Next comes a completely unscheduled stop. The driver gets out, the conductor follows suit, they meet somewhere in the middle. We listen to the rain. There are no signs anywhere. Chimneys, some stout, some slender, puff away in unrelieved torment. The rain shreds the thick smoke, pulverizes it, evenly, without rancour. The rain pulls curtains in front of the scene, curtains without ornaments. There is no landscape, just a kind of extended townscape, industrial-scape—punctuated with picturesque garden locations.

Then, barely visible through the rain, we catch a glimmering of an undertaker on one side, and on the opposite side Persil, the epitome of life. No one speaks. Each time the door opens, someone slams it shut. It's cold. When we stop, it's colder. We feel like pulling our feet up on to the seats, but that's almost certainly forbidden. We have leisure to read the notices· TWENTY SEATS; NO SPITTING. I have half a mind to.

Now we're on the move again. And here is the beginning of the next conurbation. We reach our destination. It looks like where we began from. It's as though there are no spatial destinations here, only temporal ones, like the certain, final and irrevocable death of the last patch of native earth.

Frankfurter Zeitung, 9 March 1926

9

Smoke Joins up the Towns
(1926)

Here the whole sky is smoke. It connects all the towns. It hangs in a grey pall over the land that has made it and that continues to make more of it. The wind that might scatter it is choked and buried under it. The sun that might tunnel through it is deflected and buried in thick clouds. Like something not earthborn and ephemeral, it ascends, conquers celestial regions, acquires mass, spins substance out of nothing, bundles its shadow into a body and incessantly increases its specific weight. It draws new sustenance from massive chimneys. It rises voluminously into the air. It is sacrifice, god and priest all at once. Billions of specks of dust are exhaled by it. By the mere fact of producing it, we worship it. We create it with an industry that is more than reverence. We are filled with it.

Also filled with it is the metropolis that is made up of all the towns of the Ruhrgebiet. An unholy expanse of greater and lesser conurbations, linked by rails, wires, interests and surrounded by smoke, cut off from the rest of the country. If it was just one single, great, gruesome city, it would still be a fantastic place, but not so menacingly ghostly. A big city has centres, rows of streets joined up by the sense of a structure, it has history, and its checkable expansion is somehow calming. It has a periphery, a limit, a line where it stops and goes over into country. Here, though, are a dozen beginnings; and it ends a dozen times. Land wants to resume, poor, smoke-pregnant land, but along comes a wire and says: not here you don't. Great cubes of brick factory advance unceremoniously, stand there, more firmly set than mountains or hills, more naturally decreed than woods. Every small town has its focus, its edges, its development. But since they are all to be united by smoke to a single city, the separate forms and histories lose credibility, certainly function. Why? Why? Why is Essen here? Why are Duisburg, Hamborn, Oberhausen, Mülheim, Bottrop, Elberfeld, Barmen there? Why so many names, why so many mayors, so many officials for a single town? And as if all that weren't enough, a provincial border runs through the middle of things. The inhabitants have the delusion of being Westphalians on the right, Rhinelanders on the left. But what are they really? Inhabitants of the smokeland, smoke worshippers, smoke makers, children of smoke.

It's as though the inhabitants of the cities were outdistanced by the wisdom and the aspirations of the cities themselves. Things have a better feeling for the future than people do. People feel historically, i.e. retrospectively. Walls, streets, wires, chimneys feel prospectively. People get in the way of progress. They hang sentimental weights on the winged feet of time. Each one wants his own church tower. In the meantime chimneys grow over the heads of church towers. The smoke eats up the sound of bells. It swaddles them in its black wool, so that they cannot be heard, much less told apart. Each city has its theatres, its monuments, its museum, its history. But none of these things has any lasting resonance. For historical or so-called cultural things live off the echo that sustains them. Here though is no room for echo and resonance. The sounds of bells live from echo, and they all fight each other, until the smoke comes along and chokes them.

Some of the smaller towns here have their old gabled romantic parts. These are referred to as idyllic. Time drones all round them. Busy wires enmesh them. All the trembling airwaves are full of the radio-borne words of the present. What is the point of these slumbering nooks, these dreamy beauties? While there was a blue sky over them they were in their element, but now grey smoke hangs over them. They are buried under billions of dust and carbon particles. They will never experience a resurrection. Never will a pure naked sunbeam gild them. Never will a pure rain rinse them clean. Never will an actual cloud lend them shade. In all their fixity they are doomed. They were built for the ages in lasting stone, and their durable construction is the only reason they still exist now. Not because they have any force or presence. They are like old silver coins that have no value as currency. The flimsiest banknote is more actual.

It is of just such ridiculous thin material that the new parts of cities are built. There are walls you can pinch between finger and thumb. There are tenements of wood and hollow brick. There are shingle roofs that children might have draped. Things stand and fall and are rebuilt. Moments ago they were white and gleaming with fresh paint. Now they are black as rotten teeth. Each street a gaping mouth.

People live here. People with ambitions and desires. Even the unemployed. They step out. Why hang about? What is there to see here? Children play in the middle of the streets. All the windows are identical. All the doors are identical. Only the numbers on them are different. All the people are grimly determined to reach their destination. Perhaps it is the dole office. Perhaps the co-op. Perhaps it is a meeting hall. Perhaps a break-in. Perhaps the revolution. Perhaps it is the cinema.

Oh, but it matters so little! One destination is like the other. One city like the next. Each street like the next. Climb on the tram. In half an hour you'll be in the next place. Is there any difference? Smoke over the world! You go to Oberhausen, and then Mülheim, and then to Recklinghausen, to Bochum, to Gladbeck, to Buer, to Hamborn, to Bottrop. Smoke over the world! No sky, no clouds. Rain precipitated from smoke: black rain. A hundred chimneys, so many fingers, pillars of the smoke sky, altars of the Almighty Smoke. Rails along the ground, corresponding wires through the air. All one grim city made of stacks of city, of bundles of towns. In amongst it all runs the abstract provincial boundary. But overhead is the uniform sky, and that is smoke, smoke, smoke.

Frankfurter Zeitung, 18 March 1926

10

Germany in Winter

(1923)

There is something half-hearted about this winter. The calendrical harshness of nature is nothing to the boundless cruelty of history. Snow melts away a couple of hours after falling. A mild zephyr blows over the land. There is a relation between the desires and the fears of the hungry, the cold, the unshod and the unclothed, and the permanent laws of the changing seasons. God's fist has never oppressed us so much; the hand that doles out frost and bitterness every year was never so mild. There is some compensatory mechanism.

I come from abroad, where they pack up mercy parcels for Germany's army, and where the newspapers mount withering attacks on German politicians on their front pages, but their back, human pages stick up for German victims; where the window displays of banks and exchange parlours exhibit endless Reichsmark notes, not as negotiable objects of exchange, but as curiosities; where Germany's best actors appear, not for fame, but for rustling currency; where the money still has a good oily sheen, and feels soft and smooth in the hand, as though coloured by the sacred, kingly fat of the Golden Calf.

But in this abroad the station-guard goes hungry, the trains come and go unpunctually, the heating doesn't always work, the porters haggle, the toilets don't flush, and the lighting in the compartments is wretched. Whereas in Germany railway carriages are full of embittered businessmen, and a hungry inspector checks your tickets—but the heating works, and a beaming lamp, worthy of a nice sitting room, sheds its light. The porters certainly have set fees. The timetable isn't a work of fiction. The trains actually stick to it. Officials man the counters. Water flows into the WCs. The machinery of public life is well and dependably oiled. In the cities, busy brooms whisk canine excrement into purpose-built gutters. Outside food shops stands the tidy rank and file of the great army of hungry Germans.

In Leipzig I saw a man from a firm of undertakers. He wore a gleaming top hat. He had a pomaded, uptwirled black moustache. He looked like a first-class funeral. He provoked fear and respect. Round about him gusts of eternity blew. He was a representative intercessor between this world and the next; a Middle European Charon; a splendidly ceremonial death. Only—he wasn't riding on a calèche drawn by a couple of black stallions, or in a black-lacquered automobile, not even on a tramcar; nor was he on shanks's pony. This awe-inspiring figure was mounted—on a bicycle. He pedalled. He pedalled to the cemetery and back. He sat hunched over the handlebars, and pedalled for all he was worth. His sinister black trousers bore shiny metal clips, and were bunched at the ankles, looking like umbrellas in fair weather. This distinguished apparition couldn't afford a tram ticket. All his metaphysical dread was wasted. It wasn't possible to have any respect for this agent of eternity—not on a bicycle. If I had been a corpse awaiting burial, this undertaker would have taken away all my fear of the coming assizes.

Then, in Chemnitz station, I saw a conductor eating chocolates. He had found the rest of a box of pralines in a compartment. The conductor was a gentleman in what they call the "best years", big, hairy fists, a square head, a short, squat body, and big, solid, waterproof boots. This man was wolfing down frivolous liqueur-filled confectionery, and lost all the gravity he was supposed to have as an

aspect of his profession. The conductor was eating a young ladies'
cinema nibble with a rigid, humourless expression, as though it was
the doorstop or hunk of sausage that would have accorded with his
personality. Six months ago, this conductor certainly wouldn't have
been tucking into chocolates. But today he is hungry. What to a
passenger was a frippery, to him is a necessity. If it had been a dry
crust of bread he had picked up—the effect couldn't have been
more abject. Things in Germany are at such a pass that its railway
conductors help themselves to expensive fripperies in their des-
peration. One party carelessly leaves them behind, to the other
they're a lifesaver. That's where Germany is right now.

In Dresden I spoke to a policeman. I slipped him five Czech
crowns, and they loosened his tongue. All his personal and professional grimness disappeared. A week ago, he had no money at all.
He was out of work. Unemployment support wasn't enough. He
picked up a rucksack and went out into the country—to beg. A
farm dog ripped his last pair of trousers. He patched them—with
rope, for want of thread. The stout rope had the effect of widening the tear in the trousers. Before long, the policeman will go
around clad in a rope.

These are the kind of things that happen to you in Germany.
Abroad, you read the speeches. They are unimportant. They are
rhetorical and political wrecks. They can do little harm and no
good. But then in Germany, you see a train conductor eating pralines; a rope in lieu of a pair of trousers; death on two wheels. A
clumsy foolishness attaches to these things. Their evident sym-
bolism looks like an invention. Life doesn't always take the trouble
to come up with something convincing. It makes jokes as crass as
any music hall entertainer. Who laughs about large, well-off families in Germany making their own money? And using it to buy
bread with? It's a grotesque implausibility in the column of
"other news". A dismal twopenny romance twines round death by
starvation. In the West End of Berlin I saw two high-school kids.

They were walking along the wide, busy road, arm in arm, like a pair of drunks, and singing:

> *Down, down, down with the Jewish republic,*
> *Filthy Yids,*
> *Filthy Yids!*

And passers-by got out of their way. No one stopped to slap their faces. Not out of political indignation. But because in any other country the irritation of a kid bothering the street with his half-baked politics would have provoked someone to a pedagogic measure. In Germany the convictions of high-school boys are respected. That's how law-abiding people are in Berlin. And that discipline is heading for a tragicomic ending. Whether it's a school-boy treating us to his political views on the Jewish republic or a conductor so hungry he wolfs down a box of chocolates—they are so laughable and tragic that no visitor could understand. No one understands Germany. It is *the least understood nation in Europe*.

A Japanese student in Berlin told me: when foreign students are matriculated in Berlin University, the rector Professor Roethe says, "We have accepted you, even though you are foreign. Thank God we are not dependent on your friendship ..." Do you see a connection between the hysteria of the chanting schoolboys and the speechifying professor? They are both instances of the decline of Germany. That's the way people in a fever rave. Anyone who has sat at the bedside of a sick patient will know that the hours are not all pathos and anguish. The sick man will talk all kinds of nonsense, ridiculous, trivial, unworthy of himself and his condition. He is missing the regulating consciousness.

That's just what is missing in Germany: the regulating consciousness.

Frankfurter Zeitung, 9 December 1923

11

Retrospect of Magdeburg
(1931)

I arrive before midnight. I knew it would be raining, and so it was: diligently and with conviction. Through the draped windows of the cafés streamed a yellowish light, along with muffled drums and cymbals. With a bold show of resolve that was worthy of an actual storm at sea, some customers left the cafés. The silver streetlamps on the empty streets seemed to be there more for the benefit of the rain than the homecomers. Old facades look moving, in amongst the distinctly neutral new buildings, and old street names had a ring of home to me, even though I was seeing them for the first time. Undeniably, the town moved me, before I started to take against it. How a man softens over time! The more you take in, the less you trust the evidence of your senses. Behind the impression given by things, you sense a secret hidden truth you are afraid of violating. No one is as cautious as an elderly mocker, especially when he knows how sensitive the local press and rotary club are. They will deny everything, even impressions! So let's be conciliatory. In my recollection—a few weeks have passed since my visit to Magdeburg—it has acquired a sheen of melancholy.

Magdeburg's principal street is Breite Strasse. The name has remained unchanged for a very long time. Its simple but confident assertion seems to me to speak for the good sense of the citizens of Magdeburg. Other towns would long since have given their main thoroughfare a more sonorous name. In that simple unchangingness I sense history and tradition. Germany has few streets in which the character of a historical thoroughfare has remained so clearly visible. Even so, there is a fight going on between the old constancy and the new zealotry, that "*neue Sachlichkeit*" that leaves no place, no movement, no association, no community untouched, disrupting the honest features of the preserved facades with a wilful cool boldness, with smooth, neutral, disagreeably emphatic concrete. Modern apartment blocks are simplistic; in their large windows and flat roofs, the brutal intention of putting space, light and air to work, to save money, and implacably to further the health of man, beast and machine, lives the whole rampant, improving arrogance of our time that knows no self-restraint; and the small towns, afraid they might end up behind the times, instead anticipate them, adopt their tempo, and so make a mess of their best architectural virtues. Opposite the old and really beautiful cathedral set in a dignified and pensive ring of dark green, lurks the Reichsbank building, a gruesome instance of contemporary barrack- and factory-culture, a stone slap in the face, spattered down at the feet of the house of prayer. They are just now in the process of cutting down a few trees giving their own shade in the shade of the cathedral. I would bet that within ten years the vogue for skyscrapers and tower blocks will have utterly destroyed the cathedral square and possibly the cathedral itself. Then the fine café, the Café Dom, a holy temple of ancient chess players where the smoke of innumerable cigars has magically tinted ceiling, pillars and walls, will have given way to a modern "metropolitan" cafeteria of linoleum, glass and chrome, one of those hygienic execution sites with dance music that we have nowadays.

The little booklet in which the town hall of Magdeburg is described is prefaced by an introduction from the mayor of Magdeburg. "To know our town hall is to love it!" he says.

One probably shouldn't ever take a mayor at his word. But the limited lexicon of human feeling that gives us "love" is surely unable to cope with the enormous dimensions of this town hall. The only feeling I can muster towards this newest of German constructions is awe. This town hall strikes me as a successful effort to construct a palace for the people; the attempt to orchestrate such a thing as the dignity of the masses. The least of the details of this enormous construction is calculated not to let the masses lose human dignity. Wardrobes you don't have to cluster around. Entrances and exits you don't have to fight to use, an economical excess of space, space, space, in which all possibility of panic is quenched: this is the masses being educated to self-control. Noble blond wood, no carpeting, plain red and blue velvet curtains; ceilings of silvery brown wood, horizontal bank of lights on the stage, shimmering nickel ornamentation; the biggest organ in Germany (if not the whole world), with ten thousand pipes! It's a triumph of size, number and utility. The practical is promoted to the ranks of the dignified, and dignity is confusingly close to utility.

On the quiet morning when I wander through the town hall, I am taken with the linguistic play between echo and corridor,* and I hear the exaggerated crashing echo of my footfall on the naked boards. When there are thousands going up and down the stairs on evenings of celebration and joy, then the echo surely won't sound so hollow, sorry and unfestive. Probably the wood then is just as quiet as carpets would be, it just needs one condition: that a sufficient mass of people be there to walk about on it. When there is just me, I feel like a solitary gymnast. As I leave the town hall and look at the cathedral opposite, I wonder whether I am allowed to say that actually I love carpets, and that bare boards always seem a trifle unadorned to me. I am standing in the so-called exhibition space. Almost every town in Germany now has such a space, in which the excessive numbers of fairs, the tournaments of trade and industry, are held: grassy asphalted spaces, airy filmy walls that in actual fact may have a trusty steel frame within them. So why is it that I feel closer to the fourteenth-century cathedral than to the town hall which was completed in 1927? Why? I can't tell you. Our grandchildren, of whom the mayor remarks that

---

* Echo and corridor: German allows a rather superior play on words here—*Hall und Widerhall*.

the town hall will show them what German determination was able to accomplish, may understand me better ...

And now from this excess more calculated to win my respect than my heart, let me come to a subject I am able to approach with affection: the people of Magdeburg struck me as more estimable than their new buildings. I knew no one when I got here, I knew several when I left. That speaks for the town. It's not possible to remain a stranger here for long. They were quiet, critical, warmhearted people. A few with that blessed trait of having returned home after wanting to see the world and feeling homesick that is sometimes called "humdrum" or "prosaic". No doubt it has its narrow-minded citizens, every town does. But it also accommodates a few un-bourgeois free spirits. They patronize a modern bookshop, and put on literary evenings. Yes, it even seems to me that this practical-minded, industrious, and architecturally inclined town is blessed with that sort of atmosphere in which native and stranger alike may lapse into forgetfulness and settle. The past nestles in the old buildings and blows from the Elbe port through the old part of town. The people are small-townish enough to have whims and eccentricities. The best of them have no desire to be metropolitan. They have time. The trams are reassuringly slow. The women are attractive. And the curfew hour is late.

From time to time I think of describing the "German", or defining his "typical" existence. Probably that isn't possible. Even when I sense the presence of such a thing, I am unable to define it. What can I do, apart from writing about individuals I meet by chance, setting down what greets my eyes and ears, and selecting from them as I see fit? The describing of singularities within this profusion may be the least deceptive; the chance thing, plucked from a tangle of others, may most easily make for order. I have seen this and that; I have tried to write about what stuck in my senses and my memory.

Kölnische Zeitung, 3 May 1931

Part II

Sketches

12

The Fraternity Member
(1924)

The fraternity student is the only zoological creature whose natural distribution has nothing to do with natural factors—with geography and climate—but is dependent on nations and governments. While in countries whose biological conditions are similar to those in Germany he may already have become extinct, or never even have arisen, we get him here, and in innumerable variants. (The technical name for these is *couleurs*.)

One encounters him in bars, on duelling-grounds and at nationalist meetings (such as lectures by Professors Roethe, Freytag-Loringhoven and others), also in lecture rooms. The fraternity student can be identified at a glance: the hypothesis that God created man in his own image receives a practical rebuttal by the facial markings which are called "scars". Askew on his closely cropped skull he sports a cap that would be the envy of any American messenger boy. Across his chest he wears a gaudy sash of two or three colours in which may be picked out a ringing phrase, as for example: "With God for King and country!" So he projects his innermost feelings and convictions, a slogan on two legs, nourished on beer and tradition, and kept in his paper life by the extraordinary long-suffering patience of German citizens. Since he has no contents, he lives on as a shell; a little like a paper lantern the day after a party.

In order to demonstrate the purpose of his existence all the same, he creates tumults and affrays—in the mistaken view that acoustic effects entitle one to exist. Even though this is where he betrays his outstanding past and present anachronism. His noise resembles the underworld stirrings of incompletely deceased ghosts.

Because he has slipped the bonds of time, he believes time is out of whack. Because he sleeps away the day, he only ever sees the world by night—and then often double. Therefore he fails to apprehend the dimensions of reality. Seeing ghosts, he is his very own ghost, seeming in the chime of a beer glass to hear the bells of Old Heidelberg. Drunkenness that saps others gives him strength. He lives from the mould of the past and decay. His sheen is as that of a dead body that phosphoresces at night. Even so—and because he is a corpse that history has failed to bury—he makes his way, called a career, protected from unsympathetic reality by laws and customs—to the top of the legal, political and medical professions. He pronounces sentences and prescribes castor oil. He becomes a professor and imagines he is spreading knowledge when he shares what he thinks he knows. Ideals from the nursery deck out his walls and hang in his brain. One day a young beer drinker becomes an old fart. Just as if he had never been alive, he wanders through the years, on the periphery of the world and yet thought to be a part of it, becomes grey and finally dies the death of the living, at the end of a life of the dead.

To his grieving fraternity, he bequeaths beer stein, sabre, swastika, cap, sash and whatever else he may possess in the way of student knick-knacks. Making haste to follow him, the next generation comes along, and plants their hopes, which to us are disappointments, on his grave ...

Vorwärts, 24 February 1924

13

Guillaume the Blond Negro
(1923)

The blond Negro, the self-contradiction, the living denial of his "black shame",* the manifest Negro with the blue eyes, a figure for Dinter,† I addressed on the train from Wiesbaden to Koblenz. A lot of stout citizens were on the train, and in a corner by the window sat the Negro. Did I say Negro? The man had thick lips, splendid white teeth, strong cheekbones—but also fair curly hair and eyes of forget-me-not blue. The whole carriage was staring at him. He was wearing a French army uniform and reading a book, a German book. Finally a fat gentleman, a traveller, a Tom, Dick or Harry, a helpful man who would offer unsolicited advice to anyone, and who knew the train timetable by heart, could help himself no longer. He leaned across to the blond Negro, and asked: "I say, what's that book you're reading?" The Negro replied: "It's a Sven Elvestad, just a run-of-the-mill thriller." Thus showing his superiority to the questioner, who had never heard of Sven Elvestad, and to whom a thriller was hardly run-of-the-mill.

---

* Black Shame: Roth ironically deploys the term that was used for the perceived shame of parts of the Rhineland being occupied by Black African French soldiers when Germany fell behind with reparations.

† Dinter: Artur Dinter (1876–1948), German racist writer and politician, obsessed with racial purity. The fact that his Nazi Party number was as low as 5 speaks for itself.

Now the ice had been broken, and the Negro started to speak. He spoke German. A fluent German, with a deep, pleasant, sonorous voice. He had already been in Europe for four months. He knew some of the major German cities, such as Cologne, Frankfurt, Hanover, Koblenz and Düsseldorf. He felt very much at home in Germany. People were perplexed that he was blond. When he went out for a moment, the heavy gentleman said to his neighbour: "I say, will you ask him how he got to be blond?" But when the Negro came back, no one asked him.

We both got out at Koblenz. He left the carriage with a hearty South German greeting: "Grüss Gott". A Grüss-Gott Negro. What a wonderful mixture—almost pure Aryan.

At the station in Koblenz he excited great interest. He was tall, broad-shouldered, high-hipped, a wonderful specimen. We waited together outside the left luggage office. He was leaving a heavy suitcase. I let him go first. He declined. We spent five minutes arguing about which of us should give in his case first. Things slowly escalated into a black shame. Finally we began talking personally, and this is what the blond Negro told me:

His name is Guillaume. But not just Guillaume, also Thiele. So his real name is Wilhelm Thiele, and he's a sergeant, and a member of the occupying army, and hence an enemy of Germany. A Negro and blond and blue-eyed, a bundle of contradictions. A political, an ethnological paradox.

His father was in the Foreign Legion, his mother was black. So he got the blond hair from his father, and his mother tongue is German. His mother lived in Munich for a while, as a typist in a bank. He grew up with his grandparents. He's not just German, he's Bavarian. (Sometimes he says "nit" for "nicht".)

What does it feel like being in Germany, as an "enemy", I ask him.

It had made him very happy to be in Germany. He gave occasional lectures to his comrades. He read aloud to them from

Goethe. His favourite poet is Lenau. And after a quarter of an hour I could see that not only did this Negro know far more than Hitler and the Negroes of Upper Austria, he also had a deeper and more intuitive grasp of the German character than any Professor Freytag-Loringhoven or Roethe; that in the purity of his soul this Negro Guillaume stood far above the ostensible racial purity of Dinter; and that he didn't even need his blue eyes and blond hair to be German.

He lived in a little farmhouse not far from Koblenz, and I spent the afternoon with him. He played the violin. I saw that he was slimly built, with large hands and fingers. I saw the photo of his father, a man with blond upturned moustaches. He had died in the service of France. And then I saw the picture of a young girl from Munich, who is to be his bride. Later, of course, once everything is over.

I'm afraid it will be a long time before it is all over, at least in Munich, where the white Negroes dwell and where I'm sure it's not possible to be the bride of a Franco-German blond Negro, not without being raked by swastikas.

Neue Berliner Zeitung —12 Uhr-Blatt, 28 December 1923

14

Adventurers
(1922)

1. The Captain of Köpenick

The cobbler Voigt, who passed away a few days ago, was an adventurer of small scale and surprising consequence. His contribution was to extend the lexicon of crime by a single word: "Köpenick-iad".*

It is to this coinage that he owes his survival; not the boldness of his criminal imagination. He was a stunted cobbler; his exterior alone marked him out as a butt of fortune's joke. His enterprise allowed him a further coup. He himself hadn't wanted it. It turned out that at a time of doughty militarism it had an extraordinary effect. His absurd appearance was overlooked. His orders were heard and obeyed. He proved that even the most rigid discipline is helpless in the face of stupidity.

Today his image has paled. When he died, his name flickered up again here and there. People remembered a time when fate still had

---

* Köpenick-iad: a confidence trick, as when the cobbler Voigt got into a borrowed military uniform and occupied the town hall of Köpenick outside Berlin. The subject of Carl Zuckmayer's enduringly popular tragicomedy of 1931, *The Captain of Köpenick*.

a sense of humour. The present offers no such ridiculous adventurers; only dismal, humourless ones. The exploits of the cobbler Voigt come to us from a more innocent, pre-Revolutionary era: relatively harmless pranks, with a happy ending.

To each time its own adventurers.

2. Count Schlieffen

OUR TIME BOASTS Count Schlieffen, who a few days ago was re-arrested in Hamburg.

Count Schlieffen is a bourgeois officer cadet; real name unknown. Nor can he do without his military lustre. He moves in distinguished circles in Hamburg and America, gets engaged to a singer, marries her on the strength of some false documents, is unmasked at the wedding, flees to Berlin with the help of a few left-wing politicians, and there becomes an aristocrat again. Till he returns to Hamburg, where he is finally nabbed.

He is a typical adventurer of the twentieth century; a touch of demonism, drawn to politics, origins shrouded in mystery, shading into the tragic. He is the complete hero of a revolutionary age; erotic and sentimental, played upon by war and fame, socially adept and ambitious. A profiteer of our turbulent times, dashing, but with a head for figures. Not to be defeated by border guards or lack of papers, a cool liar, cool as a film hero, and innately superior to those things that ultimately ensnare him.

He loses himself, likeably enough, in complications, because—walking talking testimony to the effect of the Eternal Feminine—he gives up his career for a woman. He is arrested on his way to the singer in Hamburg, in one final attempt to talk her round.

There was no need for him to do it. He could have lived a pampered life in Berlin, untroubled by his pursuers. But probably he loves his singer. Either that or his vanity is wounded. The fact that hundreds of people take him for a swindler bothers him little. But the fact that this woman, who once loved him, no longer trusts him, that hurts.

Count Schlieffen is no hard-boiled sinner. He is sympathetic at that point where he becomes vulnerable. His heart is his Achilles heel. One can understand "Count Schlieffen". A woman was his undoing. That's masculine.

3. Count Avalov-Bermont

THIS COUNT IS a Russian commoner who has made a career in the army, has lived in Berlin since the Revolution, and has awarded, so to speak, posthumous medals to Baltic soldiers and officers. The police have therefore extradited him.

Count Avalov is an enthusiast, not a snake. He probably believes in his title and his significance. He lives in a middling B&B in the West End of Berlin with an adjutant, who is a former officer. A visit to the "Count" is one of those grotesque experiences Berlin has to offer.

The adjutant announces you, you wait in an ante-room, the door flies open, and the adjutant announces: "His Excellency". And in clatters, rattles, jangles the lofty form of the Count, who is tall and presentable: a stately pine from the gardens of Tsarskoye-Selo.

His voice is rough and hoarse. The syllables march past, curt and clipped, and form up into companies of sentences. His speech is a military function, his gestures fictive rifle exercises.

Count Avalov believes in himself and his mission. He too can be understood as a victim of his times. The Czar has been murdered and Avalov feels compelled to represent the real Russia in the eyes of the world. He pulls on his costume as a personal demonstration against Lenin and Trotsky.

He is a brave man, no doubt, and no more dishonest to the

world than he is to himself. He wishes to be a prop of the monarchy, and so offers himself as a theatrical prop.

He is an adventurer out of self-deception. He thinks of himself as a general and Machiavelli rolled into one. All he does is pin tin medals on people.

Berlin Börsen-Courier, 8 January 1922

15

The Mother

(1922)

Yesterday the nineteen-year-old labourer Franz Zagacki was sentenced to five years in prison. He had tried to kill his mother while she was peeling potatoes, first with an axe, then by asphyxiation, and finally by stabbing her. Then, supposing she was dead, he robbed her of a wallet in her petticoats containing two thousand two hundred marks, went to a tobacconist's, paid his debts, bought cigarettes, invited his friends and his sweetheart who had helped him plan the deed to a cosy get-together in the flat of the apparently deceased woman, and went out to have himself a fun day. The mother though did not die, and the son was arrested and taken to prison for questioning.

Yesterday the mother stood in court and explained that she had forgiven her son. No sooner were the wounds healed that he had dealt her, than she was setting off to her son's prison bringing preserves and other delicacies she had forgone. Even while she lay in hospital she was trembling for the well-being of her son, and if she had had the strength and if her lust for life had not prevailed when she was near death, then she would have remained quietly under the bedding in which he had tried to asphyxiate her, in order to spare him. What was her view of her child? she was asked. Nothing but the best. Oh, it wasn't his fault, bad company had led him astray, it's always bad company that's to blame. She didn't know anything about his girlfriend, he was impressionable, but when he was younger he had been a good boy.

The mother will now be able to visit her son regularly in prison. With trembling fingers she will pack up preserves for him for Christmas and the other holidays, she will scrimp and save for her son, and her old soul will weep for him and hope. And it will be exactly as though her son was not in prison at all, but at university or abroad somewhere, or in some other kind of place that is not easy to return from for professional or some other reasons.

The mother's day is full of work and painstaking, sometimes dirty labour. But between each thing and the next, the scrubbing of the floorboards and the chopping of the kindling, there will be a brief, secretive folding of her hands. And each time she sits down to peel potatoes, as when the axe struck her, she will cry from pain; but stronger than her woe is her hope, stronger than her pain her faith, and slowly from her love of the child, like young leaves from fertile soil a kind of shy pride will sprout, without cause, she couldn't say why, not based on qualities, but simply on the fact of this boy's existence.

And each time she looks at the hatchet or thinks of it, a terrible day will loom up at her out of the past. And for all its terror it's still weaker in outline and force than the other day, approaching, when her son will come home, upright, healed, and full of regret.

Full of regret? He has nothing to regret. The others are to blame, of course! Any moment the door will open, and he'll walk in. And even though it's five years, five lots of three hundred and sixty-five days, it could be any day.

Because the mother doesn't stick to facts, she denies the solar calendar and the year.

Berliner Börsen-Courier, 25 April 1922

16

Rose Gentschow

(1924)

Rose Gentschow is the daughter of a landowner near Danzig. Her father died of paralysis of the brain. Her mother is addicted to morphine, and is in an institution. Three sisters have taken the prescribed way into middle-class life that ends with marriage to a well-situated man. Rose Gentschow too could have followed that path. She was even prepared for it by the girls' academy she attended until the age of sixteen. Then she became a secretary. A harmless event undergone by many girls on the path to material self-sufficiency left Rose Gentschow with a bad and painful illness. She was twenty-one at the time. Her mother gave her morphine to relieve her pain. She lost her job. Relatives supported her. Then she met a "friend". He sent her out on the street. She stole from the flats of gentlemen she accosted in bars, abetted by her friend. Her habit was to slip opium into the glasses they drank from. One, Hemel, a businessman, died. She had slipped a little too much in his drink. He fell off his barstool and was dead. Rose was arrested.

Today she is thirty-three. She looks younger. Hers is the deceptive youth of women who are professionally young because they live off their looks; who have experienced nothing but passion which doesn't always age, but sometimes keeps them young; whose life consists of alternating waves of ecstasy and unconsciousness;

who drown anxieties, age and illness in intoxication, and forget them in the moment. Rose Gentschow has the beguiling expression of the incurable vice girl. It comes from the faraway sins of dreams. It goes into dreamy sins. Rose Gentschow has remained slender and light. She has never known the everyday worries of the middle class that make one fat and heavy. She lives in consuming passion. But also in consuming poverty. Sometimes she had to earn money to buy her beloved morphine. She sold herself so that she could afford to intoxicate herself.

On no fewer than fifteen occasions she has tried to escape her fate. Fifteen times she went on a detoxification cure. Fifteen times she lapsed back into morphine dependency. She would have extended her life and her method to an early grave, had Hemel had a stronger constitution. That he didn't was blind chance. A stroke of fortune interrupted the activity of the lady poisoner. That's how she's referred to in the court reports. The one who is poisoned though is she. Her hands are thin, and her gestures awkward and embarrassed. She cries a lot. She tries to hide her face. Then she dries eyes and tears with a fist. The childish movement is charming. Little girls dry their tears with their fists.

She is facing three judges and six jurors. This is the composition of the new courts, following the ministerial decree of 24 January 1924. The jurors sit up alongside the judges. The jurors' bench is empty. When Rose Gentschow speaks, she speaks to nine men. She looks at them all. Sometimes her look catches on one or other of them. Perhaps he seems kinder, better, more benevolent than the others. Then the controlling consciousness corrects the stalled look, and she goes back to watching all nine.

Her voice is thin and low. With all her self-control, tears are never far away. In spite of herself, a sob catches in her throat. Sometimes she is hoarse, creaky, as though speaking without vocal cords. She sounds choked, as though she kept her hand in front of each of her words.

Her former neighbours are in attendance. They are curious and lacking compassion. It is possible they are vindictive. Naïve people often are. Some share the destiny of the accused. Morphine lurks in their eyes. Their hands shake. Do they feel they have something in common? Are they suffering with her? Are they looking into their own future? I watch them eating their sandwiches. Perhaps one can see one's destiny accomplished before one's very eyes and still feel hungry. Men are there, both as witnesses and onlookers. Their constitution survived her opium. An army officer speaks. He is as calm and objective as a lawyer. He is not at all excited. But he too was one of her victims. His constitution withstood the opium. He met the girl on Potsdamer Platz. She wasn't the first, nor the last. These are the women he crosses paths with. He doesn't become her destiny, nor she his. They are his episodes, and luckily he too is just an episode. He wanders along on the fringes of danger, and nibbles at them.

Rose Gentschow is still hoping for reprieve. But her small, fogged brain is not equal to the sharpness of the judge. He asks: "How did you come to steal?" She answers: "I didn't know what I was doing. I had already taken a lot of morphine." The judge: "Were you stealing on the orders of your friend?" She, swiftly espying possible salvation: "Yes, yes!" The judge: "Then how can you claim not to have known what you were doing?" She is baffled by the logic. From a world of inebriation and thoughtless exhaustion, she suddenly finds herself in a sphere of implacable reason. Dazzled by the luminosity of logic, she leans back, closing her eyes. She loses herself, she is lost.

She can go on no longer. The world is sinking. She opens her eyes once more. Then she lapses into a kindly oblivion.

Prager Tagblatt, 10 April 1924

17

Two Gypsy Girls
(1924)

The sun had an unusual, animating shine, it was as brisk as early morning, and as warm as noon, and lots of people were hurrying along the busy street. They were coming out of department stores carrying parcels, they were bustling about, dressed in bright and cheery clothes, as though they were on their way to a great party. The screaking trams, the tooting cars, the clattering buses were creating a joyful tumult. The whole city felt as cheerful as an adult become childish with joy.

Just then two young gypsy girls came along.

They were very brown and were wearing bright colourful clothes, red blouses and blue and white floral skirts, red ribbons in their hair and big yellow amber necklaces at their throats. On their feet they had red sandals. They had suddenly sprung up from somewhere, maybe they had come out of a shop. Even in their haste, the people stepped aside, so that they walked into an unoccupied space, and the looks that were sent their way were in equal part astonished and suspicious. They had little childish faces, pointy chins on which smiling dimples barely managed to find room, and brimming violet eyes. (Even their whites had a bluish shimmer.) Their blouses seemed to be casually unbuttoned, and yet were chastely closed, and the stout amber necklaces made their slender throats look even nobler, narrower, aristocratic. Under the flowing garments one sensed they were well-grown.

The two young gypsy girls were walking slowly, casually, a little taken aback, a little confused by the sunny throng, like a pair of alarmed young queens. Even so, their sandals barely brushed the paving stones; the teetering steps of young ladies in heels were heavier and stayed longer on the ground, even though they were in a hurry. The young gypsies wanted to cross the main road, but they were afraid of the vehicles that clattered by so merrily and dangerously to life and limb. Three times they walked out into the middle of the road, only to flee back to the pavement like alarmed colourful birds. A great panic came over their pretty faces. People laughed a little.

So I went up to the gypsies, stepped between them, took them by the arm, and led them across, feeling how they trembled.

When I got to the other side, I tipped my hat to them and let them go their ways.

A gentleman with a large blond moustache that went out into a couple of butchers' hooks threw me an angry look from his sky-blue eyes, full of contempt and menace and inexpressible rage.

The two young gypsy girls didn't turn back, they walked on. A puff of wind blew out their skirts, and they looked like two wandering flags.

Frankfurter Zeitung, 12 May 1924

18

Grock

(1924)

Grock is in Berlin. Grock, the great clown.

First of all a bespectacled gentleman in dinner jacket walks on stage. He is a violinist, a virtuoso, a ten a penny virtuoso, a civilized being, there is nothing out of the ordinary about him. As he holds the violin under his chin, lifts the bow with a graceful and practised movement and begins to play, it is all of exemplary mediocrity, unobtrusive and routine.

Then the right wall lifts quietly, and very carefully, sheepishly, and with the modest air of someone who has no business being there, a very striking creature walks onto the stage in baggy grey tails, falling too far over the baggy grey trousers, and with a round grey bowler hat on his head. The bulging eyes, which from the shape of them must be exceedingly stupid, though they have a sort of unnatural cunning, carefully test the atmosphere. A long, very soft and well-behaved chin hangs sadly down, resigned, disappointed a thousand times over, ten thousand times over, but still with a little optimism. No doubt about it: this is Grock.

Grock is carrying a large suitcase. It contains a minuscule violin. The gentleman in the dinner jacket is vastly surprised. Grock is beginning to feel at home. Oh, it's so nice being here! What a kindly gentleman! Now Grock will play you something. He settles himself on the chair arm, with his big, soft, yellow shoes on the seat, and plays very nobly, very movingly, and with plenty of feeling, proper grown-up notes on his tiny violin.

Next he is to accompany the gentleman at the piano. But first he has to change. He returns in a set of tight black tails, with pitifully bowed, wavy legs in tight, implacably form-hugging trousers. And now begins the fight against life, the brutal unremitting struggle against the resistance of everything in the world, the wickedness and unfittedness of things, the grotesque illogic of ordinary circumstance. The piano is too far from the stool: he needs to move it. The lid is open: if he tries to put his top hat on it, it will fall to the floor. It's impossible to hit the correct notes, because he is wearing thick white gloves. So he had better take them off. How is a man to come to such a conclusion unaided? Luckily, he has his sensible friend to tell him.

Grock takes off his gloves and rolls them up. They look like an egg. An egg! Did you ever?! An extremely amusing scene surfaces in Grock's memory: a man juggling with eggs. A conjuror. Just at that moment juggling seems more important than music making. A pair of white gloves in the guise of an egg leaves Grock with no option. It takes quite some time. Finally the gentleman calls him back to the piano.

Grock has a wonderful, round, almost cylindrical mouth organ. It's capable of sounding like an organ. Because of course it is a terribly dignified, positively sacred object. But when you hold it in your hands, sometimes it plays itself. It makes singular very high squeaky sounds. Grock is afraid of these sounds that seem to leap of their own accord from the interior of the instrument, exuberant little beasts, unable to stand their long imprisonment. Grock leaps away. He still has the mouth organ. A little note squirts out. Grock turns round. There is a titanic battle between the man's will, his fingers and the obstinate instrument.

Several times this fight reaches a sort of climax: when Grock starts to look for his cufflinks way past his elbow, where a normal person gets his vaccination; when Grock takes the violin in his right hand, the bow in his left, and is unable to play; when Grock tosses the bow high up in the air and is unable to catch it. Then he goes behind a partition to practise. Comes out, throws the bow in the air and catches it. A minute passes. Then Grock remembers he has pulled off his difficult trick, and he cheers, a cheer that is half grunt, half whoop. It is the great joy of an adorable idiot.

He thanks the audience for their applause, comes out in front of the curtain, bows, and then can't find his way offstage. Grock is cut off from the scenery, left to the mercy of the people in the stalls who now, of all things, applaud him—but for how long, how long? Soon, they will start to laugh at his helpless condition just as they laughed at his intentional jokes before—evil people. No one makes a move, no one shows him where to go, the curtain has innumerable pleats, yes, it seems to consist of nothing but pleats, one of them must be the way out, but which one. What an awful pickle. Mustn't show that he's stuck, whatever he does! Another nice, smiling, adorable bow. The people are to believe that he's staying out of gratitude, sheer heartfelt gratitude. Then while they're still clapping, quickly pick up the curtain, and slip under it! Saved

Grock appears once more, but it is a different Grock, a Grock without bald patch, with a sad face full of noble ugliness, an aristocrat in a crude world, a man of noble truth betrayed a thousand times, an honest, yes, a humble striver who always comes a cropper, a man born for despair who forces himself to believe, a clumsy so-and-so, a hero, a lofty man in the depths, defeated a thousand times but always victorious.

Frankfurter Zeitung, 10 December 1924

19

The Dapper Traveller

(1924)

The dapper traveller enters the compartment carrying in his hand a small case of soft leather, accompanied by a porter who hoists a suitcase of tough leather into the luggage net. The dapper traveller pays him quietly without looking and without responding to his goodbye. Straightaway he drops into the seat and bounces up once before his body comes to rest. He peels off his grey leather gloves and lays them in the soft little case, from which he takes out a pair of grey thread gloves. These he puts on, stroking each finger straight. Thereupon he looks in a mirror with leather backing, runs his right hand lightly through his hair, and looks out of the window without fixing any particular object or person.

The traveller is clad in a discreet grey, set off by an exquisite iridescent purple tie. With complacent attention he examines his feet, his leather shoes, and the fine knots in the broad laces. He stretches out his legs in the compartment, both arms are casually on the arm rests to either side. Before long the grey traveller pulls out his mirror again, and brushes his dense, black parted hair with his fingers, in the way one might apply a feather duster to a kickshaw. Then he burrows in his case, and various useful items come to light: a leather key-holder, a pair of nail scissors, a packet of cigarettes, a little silk handkerchief and a bottle of eau de cologne. Then the traveller pushes a cigarette between his lips and pats his pockets for matches. Now, where are his matches? Yes, where are they, the elegant, flat matches for his waistcoat pocket, with their little yellow youthful phosphorus heads?

They are forgotten, lost, stolen, spoiled, disappeared, they are not there. The dapper traveller no longer dominates the compartment. Yes, he even feels a little trivial, with his impeccable outfit and no matches. His distinguished, sensual, olive-yellow face takes on a pale brown coloration. With his soft little leather case in his hand, he marches off in the direction of the dining car.

When he returns, fed, a little grease at the corners of his lips, he pulls a leather-bound volume from the pocket of his travelling cloak. He writes with a silver pencil, engrossed, dreamy. He is surely a poet.

Yes, clearly, a popular poet. He invents female characters so ethereal, so morphinistically thin that one may not see that they are spun from nothing at all. He is a poet on laid paper, his hand signs three hundred and fifty-one book jackets a year.

But as he leans forward and puts his book down on his knee, I see that what he was writing and totting up were columns of figures. The beautiful book contains profane calculations.

Then he puts a cigarette between his lips and his olive yellow face turns brown, and because I am getting off soon, I offer him my matches. But he refuses them. Because mine is a common or garden matchbox, bulky, just the thing to spoil the line of a waistcoat pocket, and full of common or garden red-tipped matches, not to be carried in a leather case without compromising oneself.

Frankfurter Zeitung, 8 August 1924

Part III

Austria and Elsewhere

20

Bruck and Kiralyhida

(1919)

Bruck-Kiralyhida was once like so: hyphenated.

Then came the revolution, it washed away the hyphen, and with that the Dual Monarchy was finished.

If the hyphen had remained, we might still have had the Duality today.

The hyphen was in reality a bridge, the bridge over the Leitha, connecting cis- and trans-. Traffic crossed the bridge completely unimpeded. On this side people spoke German and Hungarian, on the other side Hungarian and German. This side they swaggered in black and yellow, the other side they glittered in red, white and green. On this side they were loyal to the emperor, on the other to Kiraly. Those were the main differences; everything else was negligible. Here as there, the children were blond, brown- or black-haired, but always dirty. Here as there, the merchants were clever, practical-minded and sober. Here as there, one could get through money easily and painlessly. And get through it one did. Nowhere in the monarchy more easily than in Bruck-Kiralyhida.

During the war there was a penal institution in Bruck that went by the name of "Officers' Training College". It had the task of turning one-year volunteers "with button" into privileged detainees with a claim to pay and an ensign's sword-knot. Every day the striplings of this institution marched across the bridge. Back then the bridge still signified the place where Austrians and Hungarians rubbed shoulders, to fight and give their lives for their joint fatherland. The ones for the Kaiser, the others for their king. Back then, it was still one person. Now one has become two. The hyphen is gone …

But no. If one looks more closely, it is still there. Only it is called something else. It has become a line of separation. Instead of conjoining, it dissevers. In a word, it is a frontier. The hyphen is an armed frontier. Defended on this side by Austrian gendarmes, on the other by Red Guards. An eerie feeling to stand close to the bridge. The heart for a moment stops beating. The end of the world. The beginning of chaos. The limits of common sense. Or of irrationality?

Frontier traffic is lively. People exchange money, goods, ideas. In the interests of fairness, the Austrian government has despatched one policeman for every Hungarian *agent-provocateur*. They get along extraordinarily well, and frequent the same bars. The better to observe the other, they play billiards together.

There are also middle-class people. Hungarian capitalists. They are very difficult to tell apart from the *agents-provocateurs*. They also speak Hungarian, are just as elegant, their wallets have the same extent and cubic volume. Only they don't dare to cross the border, and are waiting for the fall of the Kun dictatorship. The *agents-provocateurs* are waiting for the dictatorship of the proletariat to reach Austria. That's the extent of the difference.

The entente is represented as well. By four Englishmen, NCOs, on 100 crowns per diem. Only one of them speaks any German. And so the four of them hang around together all day. They eat the same food, drink the same drinks, buy the same commodities. Simply because only one of them knows any German, and so the others all fall in with him. Because it's awkward and not very English to talk a lot and to gesticulate. The Hungarians more than make up for it. They all speak German.

If you're not very careful, the shops, cafés, hotels, etc., will give you twenty kronen change in two-krone notes, with serial numbers all beginning with seven. It's an unlucky seven. The money is Kun money, and therefore worthless. The best thing to do is palm it off on a clueless traveller coming from the depths of Austria to use as tips.

As I say, Bruck is a little alarming. People here come in two types: those in blue shirts, and those in white shirts. The former are police spies, the latter communist agitators. (The locals wear no collars.) As a stranger, you come in for lots of suspicious looks. Either you're a spy or an agitator, or you decide to leave your collar behind. Then you'll be picked up by the nearest cop and your worries will be over.

Strange city! When I wanted to stretch out at night in the too-short bed, I dreamed that my nose collided with a hyphen, at the very point where the Red Guards are. I caught a whiff of Béla Kun, awoke dripping with sweat, and was unable to get back to sleep.

I will never go to Bruck on the Leitha again. Ever since it's stopped being Bruck-Kiralyhida, it's become a little edgy. And all on account of one hyphen.

It's too bad about the hyphen.

Der Neue Tag, 20 July 1919

21

Journey through Galicia: People and Place

(1924)

The country has a bad reputation in Western Europe. Our complacent culture likes to associate it with squalor, dishonesty and vermin. But while it may once have been the case that the East of Europe was less sanitary than the West, to say so today is banal; and anyone doing so will have said less about the region he claims to be talking about than the originality he lacks. And yet Galicia, one of the great battlefields of the Great War, is a long way from being rehabilitated. Not even for those to whom a battlefield is *eo ipso* a field of honour. Even though Western European bodies fell on Galician soil. Even though out of the mouldering bones of dead Tyroleans, Austrians and Germans sprouts the characteristic maize of this country.

"Kukuruza" is what they call the ears of maize. When they are ripe, they are hung round the straw eaves of the peasants' huts, large, yellow, naturally occurring tassels, fluffed with long yellow hairs. Pigs are fattened on Kukuruz, and geese and ducks, and then brought to market. Poor Jewish traders put their maize in pans of boiling water and wander through the streets with the hot kernels, to sell them to other poor Jews who trade in old rags, and leftovers of glass and newspapers. The Kukuruz dealers live off the ragmen. But who do the ragmen live off?

It's difficult to live. Galicia has more than eight million inhabitants to feed. The soil is rich, the people are poor. They are peasants, traders, craftsmen, officials, soldiers, officers, merchants, bankers, landowners. There are too many traders, too many officials, too many soldiers, and too many officers. All of them live off the only productive class, namely the peasants.

These are devout, superstitious, anxious. They live in timid awe of the priest, and have boundless respect for the "city", from which come strange horseless carriages, officials, Jews, gentry, doctors, engineers, geometers, electricity, which is known as "elektryka"; the town into which they send their daughters for them to become maids or prostitutes; the town where the law courts are, the clever lawyers a man has to be wary of, the wise judges in their gowns behind metal crosses under the colourful pictures of the Saviour in whose Holy Name a man is sentenced to months and years and sometimes even to death by the rope; the town which he feeds so that it can feed him, so that he can go there to buy colourful headscarves and aprons, the town where "commissions", decrees, local ordinances and newspapers break out.

That's the way it was under Emperor Franz Joseph, that's the way it is now. There are different uniforms, different eagles, different insignia. But the basic things don't change. Among these basic things are: the air, the human clay, and God with all His Saints that inhabit the heavens and whose images are put up by the side of the road.

These holy pictures in among the wide cornfields, on the edges of the meadows, were destroyed in the Great War, riddled with holes and hacked at and crippled and then put up again, repainted, and given inscriptions that indicate the peasants' sacrifice was as great as their devotion was profound. This is not the way everywhere. One little village in East Galicia still has that celebrated Christ whose cross was shot away, leaving only the stone Saviour, his bleeding feet nailed to a stump, his arms spread wide in incomprehension of a silent God and a trigger-happy world; a Redeemer crucified without a cross; the symbolic consequence of the odds of war. The miracle was rightly left to stand. All round it, the trenches slowly grow over.

But they leave ugly scars that are like a disfiguring skin disease of the earth. I try to avoid the kind of reportage that looks out of a railway window and jots down fleeting impressions with a rush of satisfaction. But I can't. My eyes always move from the speaking features of my fellow travellers to the melancholy flat world without limits, the mild sorrow of the fields into which the battlegrounds have grown, to subsequent details. Around me, a strange and typical man may just be explaining a world, his world— I can't take my eyes off the little station.

All these stations are small and narrow, consisting of a pavement with a couple of rails in front of it. The platform looks like a scrap of road stuck between fields. As though it was a busy street corner by a stock exchange, dark-haired and red-haired Jewish traders take up position here. They aren't expecting anyone, they aren't seeing off any friend, they are going to the station because it is part of the profession of a small trader to go to the station to watch the train come in, the passengers get out, the once-a-day train, the only connection to the world beyond, that brings with it something of the world's hubbub and something of the great deals that are concluded across the world. The train brings German-language newspapers from Vienna and Prague and Ostrava. Someone reads aloud. Later, the traders go home, talking in little groups, along the path that connects the little town to the station, fields on the left, fields on the right; on the right is the picture of Jesus, on the left a saint's shrine, and between them go the Jews with lowered heads, careful not to touch the cross, and to avoid the saint, between the Scylla and the Charybdis of the alien, deliberately ignored faith. Mud splashes up from the street.

From a distance the mud has a sheen like dirty silver. At night you might take the roads for murky rivers, in which the sky with its moon and stars is reflected a thousandfold, as in a dirty, distorting crystal. Twenty times a year they pour stones into the mud, rough blocks, mortar and rust-brown bricks, and call it ballast. But the mud comes out on top; it gulps down the blocks of stone, the mortar, the bricks, and its deceptive surface mimics something solid and flat, as whole mountain chains slumber under gurgling water, a line of hills painfully driven through narrows. Many baggage trains have flogged down these roads, gun carriages left deep tracks, the horses sank down to the saddle—I remember it, I was there. Once, I tramped down these roads and others just like them, a pack man among pack animals, and the endless mud swallowed us alive, as it swallows the ballast of the roads.

Just as a mountain river will widen out to form lakes, so the road widens out into a circular marketplace. This is where the town was born. It is an offspring of the road. There are secret laws by which a small town will be created in one place, and a village in another. The one round and wide, the other longish and slender. The market produces a hamlet, which produces a little town. It will never make a city. The careers of places are as preordained as those of men.

For it appears that in this land the conditions for development are not given. Things don't grow. They warp and distort. In this maltreated, scorned corner of Europe, the Gothic is very much alive. There are places where everything seems unreal: families living in summer from the sale of cucumber juice and in winter from saying prayers for the dead; haunted castles; small barefoot boys selling drinking water in the station, just water, nothing else. In Lemberg it happened that a big shire horse fell through an open drain cover. The drain covers in Lemberg are no bigger, the horses no smaller than in the rest of Europe. But God allows miracles to happen. Every Sunday He outdoes Himself.

A man in the small towns of Galicia is different from a man in the small towns of Western Europe. There he grows into pleasures, bounded by a glass of wine in the morning, and the cosy *Stammtisch* at night. The small town in Galicia knows no pleasures. It even turns its philistines into a phenomenon. It encourages eccentricity. The frenzy of the great cities of the world rampages through the small towns of Galicia. There is movement without discernible purpose and for no evident reason.

But the same wind keeps blowing across the flat land, though one hardly feels it. Hills, intimations of the Carpathians, ring the distance in blue. Ravens circle over the forests. They were always at home here. Since the war they have prospered. Nothing in the way of industry, advertisements, soot. In the markets people sell the sort of primitive wooden figurines that were current in Europe a couple of centuries ago. Has Europe come to an end here?

No, it hasn't. The connection between Europe and this half-banished land is vital and unbroken. In the bookshops I saw the latest literary titles from France and England. A cultured wind carries seeds into the Polish soil. Strongest of all is the line to France. Even to Germany, more obliquely situated, occasional sparks fly back and forth.

Galicia lies in unworldly seclusion and yet is not isolated; it was banished but not severed; it has more culture than one might suppose from its deficient sewage system; plenty of disorder and still more eccentricity. Many remember it from the War, but then it hid its true nature. It wasn't a nation. It was either hinterland or Front. But it has its own delights, its own songs, its own people, and its own allure: the sad allure of the place scorned.

Frankfurter Zeitung, 20 November 1924

22

The Polish California
(1928)

D ear Friend,
 I have just been to visit one of the most interesting parts of Europe, the part of Mala-Polska where the oil wells are. As you will know, it lies in Galicia, on the northern edge of the Carpathians, and its centre is the strange town of Boryslav. Oil has been produced here since the middle of the nineteenth century. The dark wooden drilling towers are positioned over an area of ten square miles or so. Compared to the towers of Baku, these seem less cruel to me, and less inimical to the earth's surface. The earth in the Caucasus clearly suffers the curse that makes up for the blessing buried beneath. There is nothing green there, only yellow-grey desert sand and dirty brown ponds that seem not to want to dry, even though everything seems condemned to dry in the southern sun. Here in Boryslav, dubbed "the Polish Baku", the sun is moderate, the drilling towers thin and rickety and in spite of their numbers still not the only things growing. There are still woods, which are slow to make room for the towers, seeming more to surround them fraternally than to flee from them in dread. One's eye moves from the planked wells to the green hills, which are rendered somewhat respectable by virtue of the fact that they are part of the Carpathians. Were it not for the dust, which really is the brother of the Caucasian dust, there would only be the towers that evoke Baku.

But there is the dust, white and extremely thick. It's as though it were not the chance outcome of rubble and dead matter, but its own element like water, fire and earth, less to do with these than with the wind, before which it spins in thick veils. It sheets the road, like flour, powder or chalk, coating every vehicle and every walker, as if it had a will or inclination of its own. It has a special relationship with the sun when it burns, as though it were fulfilling its task. And when it rains, then it turns into an ash-grey, wet, sticky mass, which forms greenish pools in every hollow.

So this is where they found oil. A few decades ago, Boryslav was no more than a village, today 30,000 people live here. A single street—four miles long—connects three places without showing any of the joins. Along the front of the houses is a wooden board-walk mounted on short stout posts. It's not possible to make a conventional stone pavement, because pipes run beneath the road, carrying the oil to the station. The gap in height between the boardwalk and the little houses is quite considerable; the pedestrian reaches or overtops the roofs and looks diagonally down into the rooms. The houses are all wood. Only occasionally a larger brick house comes along, whitewashed and stony, and breaks the sequence of crooked, mouldering, crumbling dwellings. All were built overnight: at a time when the stream of naphtha-seekers first began to flow here. It's as though the boards hadn't been hastily assembled by human hands, but the breath of human greed had blown chance materials together, and not one of these fleeting homes seems to exist for the purpose of accommodating sleeping humans, but to preserve and exacerbate the sleeplessness of excited individuals. The rancid reek of the oil, a stinking miracle, brought them here. The anomie of subterranean laws—not even predictable by geology—raised the tension of the diggers to a kind of frenzy, and the constant possibility of being a thousand feet away from billions was bound to give rise to an intoxication that was stronger than the intoxication of actual ownership. And even though they were all consigned to the unpredictability of a lottery and roulette, none of them gave in to the fatalism of waiting that was a mild prelude to disappointment. Here, at the source of petroleum, everyone believed that all it took to compel destiny was his labour; and then his zeal magnified the sorry outcome to a calamity he was no longer able to bear.

The small digger could only be freed from the intolerable cycle of hope and discouragement by the mighty hand of the greater one, and of the "societies". They were able to buy up many claims at once, and with the relative calm that is a masculine aspect of wealth, abide the whims of the subterranean element. In amongst these mighty ones, whose patience costs them nothing and who could happily plough in millions overnight to reap billions at their leisure, the medium-sized speculators inserted themselves with their moderate credit and moderate risk-proneness and so further squeezed the little adventurer. These gradually forsook their dreams. They kept their huts. Some inscribed their names over the doors and started to deal in commodities, in soap, in shoelaces, in onions, in leather. They returned from the violent and tragic realms of the hunter of fortune to the sorry modesty of the small grocer. The huts that had been built to last a few months stayed up for years and their rickety provisionality settled into something like a local character. They suggested posed photographs in ateliers or crude book jackets for Californian adventures or just plain hallucinations. It seems to me, knowing several great industrial zones as I do, that commerce nowhere has such a fantastical aspect as here. Here capitalism lurches into expressionism.

And it seems likely that the place will keep its fantastical aspect. The town is on the march, and not just in a metaphorical sense. As the old wells begin to stagnate, new ones are opened, and the dusty road sets off after the petroleum. It pushes its houses outward, turns a corner, and bounds onward to catch up with the capricious mineral. If most of the wells in Boryslav and in Tustanowice are now idle, then the drillers are hammering day and night in Mraznica. I can't help thinking this road will go on for ever, a long, white, dusty ribbon going over humps and hollows, twisty and straight, provisional and durable, as unpredictable as human fortune, and as abiding as human desire.

I will admit that the sight of this great town, consisting as it does of one street, made me forget the actual laws of its social order. For the space of a few hours I thought speculation and greed were elemental and almost mysterious. The gargoyle faces of the lust for profit, the everywhere tense atmosphere, in which overnight catastrophes are a continual possibility, roused my interest in the literary possibilities of the milieu more than the actual beings that lived there. The fact that there were workers here and officials, cabbies and unemployed, tended to disappear behind the novelistic aspect of individuals. Imagination was livelier than conscience.

At least the oil workers are considerably better off than coal miners. They are specialists, even here. The average wage of an assistant is nine zloty, or four marks fifty, for an eight-hour day. A foreman gets twelve zloty. Conditions are relatively tolerable. Work is in—if not an airy space, at least one that is aired—and the smell of oil is not unpleasant, and even said to be good for the lungs. To the layman the tools used in drilling are disappointingly primitive. Motors drive the drills. A man walks round and round a sort of basin with a horizontal iron pole in his hand. The movement and the action look straightforward, but it may be a lot harder in practice. Experts say that the art of the worker lies in judging the degree of difficulty, or if you prefer, sensing the resistance to the drill of various types of geological terrain. The worker's hand must have a pronounced sensitivity, given that it stands in for the eye, which is not involved in drilling. If the borehole is choked by some object, as for instance a broken screw, then clever and cunning means are used to remove the obstacle—there are instruments of canny reach and clutch that feel in the dark. Their endeavours remind me of efforts to extract a cork from some narrow-necked container. It can cost you hours and months and money.

Money, money, lots of money! Consider that to drill to a depth of a mile costs maybe 90,000 dollars. Neither you nor I will ever own an oil well. It's become a lottery for people who basically don't need it, for banks and consortia and American billionaires. The people who once experienced the sensation of fortune bubbling up out of the ground, have already lost the capacity to feel happiness from material gain. There is a certain opposition between the fairy-tale way the earth gives up treasure, and the share-holdings of the naphtha diggers, and the stoic calm with which they await the miracle. These poor treasure diggers sit a very long way away from the miracle of nature, in the great metropolises of the West, and the fact that they are so far away, mighty, invisible and almost impersonal, gives them the lustre of godhead, directing the efforts of engineers and worker teams with mysterious glory. By far the greater part of the Polish sources is in the hands of foreign financiers. The workforces are paid out of a mystically replenished exchequer. Far away, on the great trading floors of the world, the shares are bought and sold, and transactions concluded according to opaque laws. The being and becoming of heavenly bodies are better understood by astronomers than changes in ownership by the local managers and people in charge of the wells. The petty officials can only sit there trembling when the noise of the great tempests on the world markets reaches their ear. Only recently, three large enterprises, "Fanto", "Nafta" and "Dombrowa", were sold to a French conglomerate. There was a meeting in Paris, and three or four gentlemen took out their pens and scrawled a signature, nothing more. In Boryslav and environs though, it means 500 employees thrown out of work, and hunger peers in at their windows, and rattles the doorknobs, because some god in Paris said the word: Efficiencies! And because it was a French god—and not as it might have been, a British one—diplomatic motives are woven into the lamentations of the alarmed Polish newspapers. Sceptics claim to understand that the new owners are only interested in the coup on the market, and in selling on the shares at a higher price, and not the exploitation of the resources at all. Even for optimists, though, gods are less than reliable, and at least as remote from any social feeling as from their workers and officials.

I left the area on a peaceful golden evening that gave no indication of the type of terrain that lay beneath. The workers trudged home with the serenity of peasants coming home from the fields, and it was as though they carried scythes over their shoulders, as their grandfathers before them had done. A few paupers stood by murky puddles and scooped up oil in tin canisters. They were the minor colleagues of the great French Dreyfus. Their tools are buckets, not shares. Such oil as they find they sell in minute quantities or they use it to light their temporary hovels with. That's all that a lavish nature has accorded them. Their huts stood crooked, brown and humble in the flat gleam of the sun. They seemed to huddle together a little more, to grow small, and to almost disappear completely. By tomorrow they wouldn't be there anymore.

I hope, my dear friend, that I have managed to give you some sense of the atmosphere in this Polish California. I chose to write about it to prove to you that I am not exclusively wedded to idylls in this country.

I remain your humble servant,

J.R.

Frankfurter Zeitung, 29 June 1928

23

Hotel Kopriva

(1923)

In P. is the "Hotel Kopriva". It has eighty rooms on two floors. It has a front-of-house manager who doubles as room-service waiter and porter. He is short and frail-looking and not really imposing enough to serve in a hotel of two storeys and eighty rooms. He meets guests at the station. If the town of P. had a larger station concourse, as would befit a town that harbours within itself a hotel like the Kopriva, then one wouldn't even be able see him He owes his visibility entirely to the dimensions of the station hall in P. and the anxious visitors, looking where they may sleep.

The "Hotel Kopriva" is almost always full. And yet, one almost always finds room in it. There are hotels in which the law of solid geometry is suspended and replaced by another law, which goes as follows: "A room that already has one traveller in it may under certain circumstances accommodate a second." It is to this law that the "Hotel Kopriva" owes its wealth; and to the circumstance that it doesn't show itself to its visitors first, its unchallenged standing. Many hotel managers could learn from it. Complaints do not exist where they cannot be made. There is no such thing as inaudible dissatisfaction. It is true to say therefore that all its guests are fully satisfied with the "Hotel Kopriva".

Other hotels have glossy, exchangeable names. They are called things like the Imperial, the Savoy, the Grand, the Central, the Paris, or the Metropole. But this hotel is called plainly and confidence-inspiringly: the Kopriva. Other hotels have had eighty or eighty-odd rooms. But the "Hotel Kopriva" has one hundred and twenty beds in its eighty rooms; because of the eighty, forty are "dual occupancy".

Now, dual-occupancy rooms in towns where lovers or, on occasion, married couples stay are a necessity. But in the town of P. and in the "Hotel Kopriva" in particular where almost exclusively single, rivalrous, anxious travellers put up, dual-occupancy rooms give rise to awkward scenes. The conviction that one does not snore depends on the physiological impossibility of listening to oneself in sleep; the belief that others do follows an old tradition. But an even stronger objection to dual occupancy is the prejudice that a man of distinction should and must sleep alone. So there are repeated productions of the following scene:

"I always sleep alone. On principle!"

"Whose are those things? You told me you had a room! You don't have a room at all!"

"But there is the room!"

"I'm not paying for a room with two beds!"

"Nor am I!"

"You will pay for it both together!"

"No!" said simultaneously by both visitors.

But the porter, who understands the pliancy of human nature, says: "All right then, room seventy-six."

"Unbelievable!" say both travellers. One would think they really didn't like each other. But the imagination of the porter in seeing them as sleeping companions has made them into such. Their hostility to the idea welds them together.

"Er—do you snore?" asks the first.

"I beg your pardon!" replies the other.

"I hasten to say, I don't ... !"

"You know—I don't mean this in any way personally—but I can't stand snoring!"

"That's exactly what I say! Once, I was on my way to … " And there follows the obligatory anecdote that ushers in friendships and firms up alliances.

More noxious meanwhile than any snoring is the blaring gramophone. Downstairs, somewhere in the dining room it scratches out marches, waltzes and two-steps with the inert implacability of a machine. Its insidiousness lies in the fact that its sound becomes clearer and more penetrating the further you stand from its funnel. This well-established characteristic of physics leaves the sleepless guest convinced that intervention is impossible, an illusion. Its range is limitless. The acoustic persecution is more traumatically effective in the remotest room on the second floor than anywhere on the first. It would be easier to find sleep in the sonorous throat of the funnel itself than in the illusory, delusory distance.

Sometimes there are fairs in P. It is never possible to anticipate them. They occur like natural catastrophes. They break out like storms. And then the rooms cost more. In fact, they cost twice as much. Also the fairs are surreptitious. There is no sign of them on the evening of one's arrival. You get tangled up in a fair as in a waiting net.

Thousands of sample cases wander through the "Hotel Kopriva". Its beds house commercial travellers of every kind. They sit at the single long table in the dining room. The traveller in children's toys with the doleful face. He looks like someone who should be travelling in sacred relics. But no, he carries with him the gaudy joys of life: red wooden horsemen; yellow silk clowns; bouncy monkeys on thin elastics; colourful spinning tops; chimneysweeps no bigger than Tanagra figurines, with eyes that open and close; little black devils with tongues of flame; abacuses strung with wooden beads that convert mathematics to a game. But beside him the traveller in soaps at least is cheerful. He smells of musk, patchouli, powder. The paper seller plays solitaire. The man with the fountain pens is a little old-fashioned, he reminds you of goose quills. Tobacco smoke hangs under the ceiling. And no one has any time. Everyone is between arrival and departure. The "Hotel Kopriva" is always between trains. Its eighty rooms and hundred and twenty beds whirl round and round. The "Hotel Kopriva" doesn't exist. It merely seems to exist. The gramophone tumbles upstairs and down. The sample cases fly through the air. The manager rushes from room to room. The room-service waiter runs to the train. The porter is knocked for six. The manager is the room-service waiter. The porter is the manager. The room-service waiter is the porter. The room numbers are departure times. The clock is a timetable. The visitors are tied to the station on invisible elastics. They bounce back and forth. The gramophone sings train sounds. Eighty makes a hundred and twenty. A hundred and twenty rooms trundle through eighty beds.

Prager Tagblatt, 4 December 1923

24

The All-Powerful Police
(1928)

At the end of two days I have taken against the porter of my Roman hotel. His professional friendliness is vitiated with that ill-concealed curiosity that betrays the mediocre spy. He simply wasn't born to serve the police. He has been in the hotel business for twenty years—if I can believe anything he says—and he was a hotel porter when visitors in Italy were merely guests, and not yet objects of official scrutiny. A change in regime is something a traveller sees first in a hotel porter. His first move after welcoming the guest is to ask for his passport. I will admit, I have a deep suspicion of states that demand the surrender of your passport in a hotel. (Some travellers are less particular in this regard.) All the traditional hospitality of a country that has been getting by on tourism for many years, and seems likely not to be able to get by without it for many more, becomes suspicious to me when hotel personnel start to behave in a semi-official capacity and take away my passport, and thereby my freedom of movement, even if it's only for half a day. But the hotel porter does more. When I go to him for stamps, he takes the trouble to read the names of my addressees. So concerned is he for my comfort that he will not let me walk a few steps to the letter box. He insists on posting my letters himself. The outcome is that they arrive a day or two later than they should have done.

He has some curious friends, my hotel porter. Several times a day one sees him in the company of two or three gentlemen who are certainly not guests at the hotel. Curious fellows, who, as I hand in my key, straightaway fall into a deep silence. As I walk away, I feel their glances boring into my neck. Sometimes I run into one or other of them in a café, whom just half an hour ago I heard sharing a silence with my hotel porter. Haven't we met somewhere before? Aha!

I know there are travellers who have eyes only for the ruins, and who are prepared to let spies be spies. But my sensitivity, nurtured and developed by stays in police states—which is to say, states with an anxious police—is such that no amount of tourist attractions is enough to distract me from the lively espionage culture.

When I call on the gentleman my friend in Milan recommended me to, the janitor looks me up and down. This gentleman, a businessman and devout Catholic, was under police suspicion for a time. As we leave the building together he greets the porter, to whom he sometimes gives tips, with a smile and a tad too politely. "The man is dangerous," says my host. "He could report me any moment." "What for?" "Who knows?"

Indeed, one may not know why one incurs the suspicions of the janitor and the intimate of the police. The bourgeois lives in permanent dread of incurring suspicion. The law surrenders him entirely into the hands of the police. Here, perhaps a little excursus on the helplessness of the citizen in present-day Italy.

According to Mussolini himself (as of 26 May 1927), Fascist Italy has: 60,000 gendarmes, 15,000 policemen, and a 10,000-strong rail, post and communications militia. In addition to these there are the frontier militia and a 300,000-strong volunteer Fascist militia for "national security".

The mere existence of these units would be sufficient to trim the freedoms of the Italian citizen. But then there are Fascist laws, which are such as to completely destroy them.

The Italian is not allowed to travel in his own country unless he carries with him a *carte d'identité* issued by the police authority of his regular abode. Without it, no hotel is allowed to take him in. (He will even be turned away by hospitals.) Leaving the country is a near-impossibility. The authorities issue no passports for abroad. A twenty thousand lire fine and a minimum of three years in prison is the punishment for anyone caught trying to cross the border without a passport.

Further, Italy has the concept of a so-called citizen "of ill repute". A citizen of this kind has no personal freedoms. He is under constant supervision. The police tell him when he may leave his flat. A police commission is empowered to tell him where he has to live—anywhere in Italy, or the colonies. The police, and they alone, determine his day, his work, his constitutional, his siesta, his sleep. Mussolini's explanation for this measure goes: "We remove these individuals from normal society in the same way as doctors isolate patients with infectious diseases."

To extend the dictator's simile: one would suppose that the isolation of someone struck down with anti-Fascism would be sufficient, and let the healthy do as they please. Alala! Not so! Every public event— whether of a scientific, sporting, or even charitable nature— must give at least one month's notice to the prefect of police. He must approve the time and place. He is allowed to ban the event. A commission advises him on the course to take. And who sits on this commission? The secretary of the Fascist League of the province in question and next to him the "Podesta"—the commandant of the garrison! Professors, civil servants, students and high school pupils are disbarred from associating in any way—not even for scholarly purposes. (Neither czarist nor contemporary Russia has laws like that.) Not even a memorial service may be held without police permission. The police reserve the right to determine place and time of any public meeting. And it isn't hard to imagine that where the police, for certain reasons, finds itself unable or unwilling to ban something outright, it will still set a time and a place that will make the meeting impractical or ineffectual in advance.

You understand why my host goes in fear of his janitor. The janitor has become, by police practice, a sort of conduit of opinion. The law is aware of citizens "generally regarded as of ill repute", and the catspaws of these laws are unable to walk into buildings and listen and hear the sources of this ill repute for themselves. They rely instead on tale-bearers. From the time of Metternich, janitors have been the eyes and ears of the police.

The Italian citizen goes in fear of the newspaper vendor on the corner, the cigarette seller and the barber, the porter and the beggar, the neighbour in the tram, and the conductor. And the cigarette seller, the barber, the neighbour, the traveller and the conductor are all afraid of one another. When I asked my friend, in a café in Milan on the day of Nobile's arrival, not expecting a serious reply and really only to break his gloomy silence: "What do you think of Nobile then?" he promptly replied: "I take no interest in politics." "You mean the North Pole?" "No," he insisted, "in politics." And he opened his newspaper and immersed himself in an article about military manoeuvres.

I have been browsing in Mussolini's speeches, and the following passage caught my eye: "I want you to be convinced that in Fascist Italy every minister and every secretary of state is nothing but a soldier. They will go wherever their commander orders them, and when I tell them to stay, they stay." I look up, and catch a familiar face. Two tables away from me, with a floppy red and white necktie on his chest, a sleekly pomaded head craning forward to listen, a thin cane on the chair beside him, a hand with flashing pink nails dangled over the chairback, a cowardly smile that he thinks is engaging—there is the friend of my hotel. He has picked up that we are talking in a foreign language. What an important moment. In return for two lire fifty he will tell the police about it. Alala!

Frankfurter Zeitung, 11 November 1928

25

Where the World War Began
(1927)

The World War began in Sarajevo, on a balmy summer afternoon in 1914. It was a Sunday; I was a student at the time.
In the afternoon a girl came round. Girls wore plaits in those days.
She was carrying a large yellow straw hat in her hand, it was like
summer coming to call, with hay, grasshoppers and poppies. In her
straw hat was a telegram, the first special edition I had seen, crum-
pled and terrible, a thunderbolt on paper. "Guess what," said the
girl, "they've killed the heir to the throne. My father came home
from the café. But we're not going to stay here, are we?"

I didn't manage to be quite as deadly serious as her father who
had left the café. We rode on the back platform of a tram. Out in
the suburbs there was a place where the tram brushed past some
jasmine bushes that grew close to the track. We drove along, jingle-
jangle, it was like a sleigh-ride in summer. The girl was light-blue,
soft, close, with cool breath, a morning on an afternoon. She had
brought me the news from Sarajevo, the name was visible over her,
picked out in dark red smoke, like an inferno over a clueless child.

A year and a half later—strange how durable love could be in
peacetime!—there she was again, at the goods station, surrounded
by smoke, platform two, music was blaring out, wagons screeched,
locomotives whistled, little shivering women hung like withered
wreaths on green men, the brand new uniforms smelled of finish,

we were an infantry company, our destination secret, but thought to be Serbia. Probably we were both thinking of that Sunday, the telegram, Sarajevo. Her father hadn't been to a café since, he was in a mass grave.

Today, thirteen years after that first shot, I am seeing Sarajevo. Innocent, accursed city, still standing! Sorry repository of the grimmest catastrophes. Unmoved! No rain of fire has descended on it, the houses are intact, girls are just going home from school, though plaits are no longer in fashion. It's one o'clock. The sky is blue satin. The station where the Archduke arrived, Death waiting for him, is some way outside the city. A wide, dusty road, part-asphalted, part-gravel, leads off to the left into the city. Trees, thickly crowned, dark and dusty, leftovers from a time when the road was still an avenue, are now irregularly sprinkled along its edge. We are sitting in a spacious courtesy bus from the hotel. We drive through streets, along the river bank—there, that corner there is where the World War began. Nothing has changed. I am looking for bloodstains. They have been removed. Thirteen years, innumerable rains, millions of people have washed away the blood. The young people are coming home from school; did they learn about the World War, I wonder?

The main street is very quiet. At the top end of it is a small Turkish cemetery, stone flowers in a small garden for the dead. At its lower edge an Oriental bazaar begins. Just about the middle of it, facing one another, are two big hotels, with café terraces. The wind browses indifferently through old newspapers and fallen leaves. Waiters stand by at the doors, more to verify than to assist the tourist trade. Old policemen lean against the walls, recalling peace, the pre-War. One has whiskers, a ghost of the old double monarchy. Very old men, probably retired notaries, speak the army German of Austrian days. A bookseller deals in paper and books and literary journals—mostly for symbolic purposes. I pick up a Maupassant from him (although he has Dekobra in stock as well) for a night ahead on a train without a wagon-lit. We get to talking. I learn that literary interest has ebbed in Sarajevo. There is a teacher who subscribes to a couple of literary weeklies. (It's good to know that such teachers still exist!)

In the evening, there's the *passeggiata* of the lovely, chaste women. It's the *passeggiata* of a small town. The beautiful women walk in twos and threes, like convent girls. The gentlemen are continually doffing their hats, people here know each other so well that I feel a threefold stranger. I might almost be watching a film, a historical costume drama, where the people don't know each other, the scenes of their greetings have been left in the cutting room, I am a stranger among strangers, the auditorium is dark; only the bright, garish intervals frighten me. It might be good to read a newspaper, to discover something about the world I have left behind in order to see something of the world.

By ten o'clock everything is quiet, there's the distant glimmer of a single late bar down a side street; it's a family gathering. Across the river, on the Turkish side, the houses climb up in flat terraced trays, their lights dissolve in the fog, they remind me of the wide staircase to a lofty altar.

There is a theatre and opera, there is a museum, hospitals, a law court, police, everything a city could want. A city! As if Sarajevo were a city like any other! As though the war to end all wars hadn't begun here in Sarajevo! All the monuments, all the mass graves, all the battlefields, all the poison gas, all the cripples, the war widows, the unknown soldiers: they all came from here. I don't wish destruction upon this city, how could I? It has dear, good people, beautiful women, charming innocent children, animals that are grateful for their lives, butterflies on the stones in the Turkish cemetery. And yet the War began here, the world was destroyed, and Sarajevo has survived. It shouldn't be a city, it should be a monument to the terrible memory.

Frankfurter Zeitung, 3 July 1927

26

The Opened Tomb
(1925)

In cinema newsreel footage you can see the Russian czar and the Imperial family on one of their last outings in Petersburg, the czarina, the little czarevich, the whole court, the rigid Honour Guard. This sequence is followed by the recording of the May Day parade which was recently taken by Trotsky in Moscow. Through the distance between these two slices of history the audience begins to understand how much has happened.

It should have been reversed: first the scenes with the red multitudes, under the command of a man with no military education and whose orientation is primarily literary, and then the last czar with his family. Following the picture of the czar the screen should be left white, clear and white as a funeral shroud, and a rigid silence must overlay it, compared to which the silence of the Siberian taiga would be noisy commotion. For not even an ignorant and insentient screen can show the scenes of these ten by ten dead, and more-than-dead people without emotion; this vision of ghosts who were dead at the moment they were filmed fresh and frolicsome, and who when they were murdered were not murdered; what was extinguished in them was not life so much as an unreality which bore an uncanny resemblance to life. The last czar ruled, banished and executed; he permitted branding, looting and killing in his name. Yes, he was even wound up for the piece of film. But, as the film shows, he didn't live. Even graves have a breath. This blew so deceptively through the bodies of the czar's family that one supposed they were all alive, the Archduke, the Archduchess, the rigid Guard and the little czarevich.

In the van strides the czar. He is wearing a richly stitched and braided tunic, a kind of hussar's uniform, and his face is mounted on a pointed little imperial beard screwed to the middle of his chin. His heavy eyelids are like lowered blinds. Their glassy regard is probably levelled at the camera. It's like the stare down the barrels of rifles a few years later. The czar walks briskly, with the movements of a creature that is part puppet, part shadow. He vanishes half-right, there where the white screen bleeds into black background. Not for an instant do you think a piece of film has come to an end in the projector behind you. This is the invocation of an undead soul at a spiritist séance.

The czarina and all the court ladies are wearing the fashions of the pre-War age, the big hats with wide rims, bent down at the front and up at the back, secured to the lofty coiffures by means of pins to keep them from swaying. The hats are worn at an angle and shade one profile, in order to show the other quite unprotected. They look terribly bold; they have the false boldness of robber hats at mask balls, the futile coquetterie of a scent that would be alluring but is only musty. The dresses are long and closed at the top, whalebone rings the throat like a closely fitted garden fence, and the bosom, at once respectable and emphatic, arches under a great deal of impenetrable material. The hair is pulled painfully up behind the ears.

These ladies are even older and deader than the Hussars' uniforms. They sashay past in a swift gaggle, and although they are all clad in white, they look like so many mourning veils.

It's all over in three minutes. It's no more than one of the numerous terrible moments of world history that show crowned heads at play. This one happened to have been caught by a camera and handed down to posterity. The film is a little worn, the pictures flicker, but one can't say whether it is punctures made in it by the tooth of time, or molecules of natural dust that have shrouded these seemingly living subjects. It is the most terrible irreality that film has ever shown; a historical dance of death, an opened tomb that once looked like a throne ...

Frankfurter Zeitung, 31 December 1925

27

His K. and K.*
Apostolic Majesty
(1928)

There was once an Emperor. A great part of my childhood and youth happened under the often merciless lustre of His Majesty, which I am entitled to write about today because I was so vehemently opposed to it then. Of the two of us, the Emperor and me, I came out on top—which isn't to say that I should have done. He lies buried in the Kapuzinergruft, and under the ruins of his crown, while I, living, stumble about among them. Faced by the majesty of his death and its tragedy— not his—my political convictions are silent, and only memory is awake. No external occasion has wakened it. Perhaps just one of those hidden, inner, private things that sometimes cause a writer to raise his voice, without him caring whether there is anyone listening to him or not.

When he was buried, I stood, one of the many soldiers of his Viennese garrison, in my new field grey uniform that we were to go

* Majesty: between 1867 and 1915, the Habsburgs were Emperors of Austria (the Holy Roman Empire) and Kings of Hungary—*kaiserlich* (imperial) and *königlich* (royal). This gave rise to the designation 'Dual Monarchy', the emblem of the double-headed eagle and the abbreviation "k. and k.", sometimes jocularly— as by Robert Musil—termed "Kakania".

to war in a few weeks later, a link in the long chain that lined the streets. The shock that came from understanding that the day was an historic one encountered a complicated sadness about the passing of a fatherland that had raised its sons to opposition. Even as I was condemning it, I already began to mourn it. And while I bitterly measured the proximity of the death to which the dead Emperor was sending me, I was moved by the ceremony with which His Majesty (and this was Austria-Hungary) was being carried to the grave. I had a clear sense of the absurdity of the last years, but this absurdity was also part of my childhood. The chilly sun of the Habsburgs was being extinguished, but it had at least been a sun.

The evening we marched back to barracks in our double rows— parade march on the wider streets—I thought about the days a childish piety had led me to seek out the physical proximity of the Emperor, and I mourned the passing not of the piety but of those days. And because the death of the Emperor spelt the end of the country and of my childhood, I mourned Emperor and fatherland as my childhood. Since that evening I have often thought about the summer mornings when I would go out to Schönbrunn at six, to watch the Emperor's annual departure for Bad Ischl. The war, the revolution and my radical politics could neither deface nor eclipse those summer mornings. I think those mornings were responsible for my susceptibility to ceremony, my capacity for reverence at religious occasions, and the parade on the 9 November in Red Square in the Kremlin, before every moment of human history whose beauty accords with its grandeur, and each tradition that at least confirms the existence of a past.

Those summer mornings often fell on a Sunday; as a matter of principle, it never rained. The city had laid on extra trams. Many people went out for the naïve purpose of providing a send-off. In a curious way the very lofty, very distant and very rich trilling of larks combined with the hurrying strides of hundreds of people. They went along in shade, the sun just grazing the second floor of the buildings and the crowns of the tallest trees. A damp chill emanated from the ground and the walls, but above us the summer air was already palpable, so that we felt spring and summer simultaneously, two seasons coincidentally instead of sequentially. The dew was still shining and already evaporating, and the lilac came over the garden walls with the fresh vehemence of a scented wind. The sky was a taut, bright blue. It struck seven from the church tower.

Just then a gate opened, and an open carriage slowly rolled out, high-stepping white horses with lowered heads, an impassive coachman on a terribly high box in the yellow-grey livery, the reins so loose in his hand that they dangled over the horses' backs, and we couldn't understand why they trotted so briskly, since they obviously had leave to go at their own pace. The whip was disregarded, an instrument not even of exhortation, much less chastisement. I began to sense that the coachman had other powers at his command than his fists, and other means than reins and whip. His hands, I should say, were two dazzling white spots in the midst of the shady green of the avenue. The large and elegant wheels of the coach, whose frail spokes resembled whirring conductor's batons, a children's game and an illustration in a book, these wheels completed a few mild turns on the gravel, which remained silent, as if it had been fine milled sand. Then the coach came to a stop. None of the horses moved so much as a foot. An ear may have twitched, but even that will have struck the coachman as unseemly. (Not that he moved to remonstrate.) But the distant shadow of a distant shadow moved across his face, convincing me that his ire wasn't from him but from the atmosphere above him. All was still. Midges danced in the treetops, and the sun grew gradually warmer.

Uniformed policemen, who until now had been on duty, suddenly and silently disappeared. It was among the coolly calculated orders of the old Emperor that no armed official was to be seen in his vicinity. The plainclothes police wore grey caps instead of the usual green, so as to avoid detection. Committee members in top hats with yellow and black ribbons maintained order, and kept the affection of the people within decorous bounds. The crowd too didn't dare move a foot. Sometimes we heard its muffled muttering, it was like choral praise. Still, there was a feeling of privilege and intimacy. Because it was the Emperor's habit to leave for the summer without pomp, and early in the morning, in that hour when the Emperor is at his most human, the one in which he has just quit bed and bath and dressing-room. Hence the low-key livery of the coachman, no more than the coachman of a rich man might have worn. Hence the open carriage, with no seat at the rear. Hence no one on the box but the coachman himself, while the carriage was standing by. It wasn't the Spanish ceremony of the Habsburgs, the ceremony of the Spanish midday sun. It was the minor Austrian ceremony of an early morning in Schönbrunn.

But just because this was so, his lustre was the more readily discernible, and it seemed to be personal to the Emperor and not from the laws that hedged him about. The light was modest, which made it visible rather than dazzling. We could, so to speak, see to the heart of the lustre. An Emperor in the morning, going on his summer holiday, in an open carriage, without retainers: an Emperor *tout privé*. A human majesty. He was leaving behind the business of government and going on holiday. Every cobbler could imagine it was himself giving the Emperor permission to go away. And because subjects bow most deeply when they imagine they are giving their master something, this morning found his people at their most submissive. And because the Emperor was not separated from them by any ceremonial, they themselves made up their own ceremonial in the privacy of their hearts, in which everyone placed themselves and the Emperor. They hadn't been invited to Court. So each one invited the Emperor to Court instead.

From time to time we felt how a shy, distant rumour arose, without the courage to make itself public, but just entertaining the possibility of an "airing". Suddenly it seemed the Emperor had already left the palace, we seemed to feel how he received the declamation of a poem from an infant, and in the same way as the first intimation of a still distant storm is a wind, so the first thing one sensed of the approaching Emperor was the grace that wafts ahead of majesties. Shaken by it, a couple of the committee gentlemen went into a little tizz, and from their excitement, as on a thermometer, we read the temperature, the state of things that were going on within.

At long last, the heads of those standing at the front were uncovered, and those standing further back felt suddenly restless. What was this? Disrespect? By no means! Only their awe had become a little curious, and was eagerly looking about for an object. Now they scraped with their feet, even the disciplined horses pinned back their ears, and then the most unbelievable thing happened: the coachman himself pursed his lips like a child sucking a sweet, and so gave the horses to understand that they were not allowed to behave like the people.

And then it was really the Emperor. There he was, old and stooped, tired after the poem declamations and already a little rattled, so early in the morning, by the display of loyalty on the part of his people, perhaps also a little journey-proud, in that condition that the newspaper reports were pleased to refer to as "the youthful freshness of our monarch", and with that slow old man's step that was called "supple", almost tippling along and with gently jingling spurs, an old and slightly dusty black officer's cap on his head, as might have been worn at the time of Radetzky, no higher than four fingers' width. The young lieutenants scorned this design of cap. The Emperor was the only one in the army who kept so rigidly to the rules. Because he was an Emperor.

An old cloak, lined with a dull red, enwrapped him. The sabre dragged a little at his side. His diligently waxed and polished cavalry boots shone like dark mirrors, and we saw his narrow black trousers with the wide red general's stripe, unpressed trousers, that in the old way were of a tubular roundness. The Emperor kept raising his hand in salute. He nodded and smiled. He had the look in his eye of someone who seems to see nothing in particular and everyone in general. His eye described a semicircle like the sun, scattering beams of grace to all who were there.

At his side walked his adjutant, almost his age but not so tired, always half a step behind His Majesty, more impatient and probably very nervous, impelled by the deep desire that the Emperor might already be seated in his carriage and the loyalty of his subjects have come to a natural end. And as though the Emperor weren't heading towards his carriage, but were perfectly capable of losing himself somewhere in the throng, were it not for the adjutant, he continued to make tiny inaudible comments in the ear of the Emperor, who after every whisper on the part of the adjutant, seemed to turn his head very slightly away. Finally they had both reached the carriage. The Emperor sat and issued greetings in a smiling semicircle. The adjutant walked round the back of the carriage and sat down. But even before doing so, he made a movement as though to sit not at the side of the Emperor but facing him, and we could clearly see the Emperor move something away to encourage the man to sit at his side. At that moment a servant appeared with a blanket, which was slowly lowered over the legs of both old men. The servant turned sharply, and leaped up onto the box, alongside the coachman. He was the Emperor's personal valet. He too was almost as old as the Emperor, but as lissom as a youth; service had kept him supple, just as ruling had caused his master to age.

Already the horses were pulling, and we picked up the silver sheen from the Emperor's dundrearies. The crowd shouted their "Hurrah!" and "Long Live the Emperor!" At that instant a woman plunged forward, and a piece of paper fluttered into the carriage like a consternated bird. A petition! The woman was seized, the carriage stopped, and while plainclothes policemen took her by the shoulders, the Emperor smiled at her, as though to allay the pain the police was doing her. And everyone was convinced the Emperor didn't know the woman would be locked away. Meanwhile she was taken to a police station, questioned, and released. Her petition would have its effect. The Emperor owed it to himself.

The carriage was gone. The even clopping of the hooves disappeared in the shouting of the crowd. The day had turned oppressively hot. A heavy summer's day. The clock on the tower struck eight. The sky was a deep azure blue. The trams jingled. The sounds of the world awoke.

Frankfurter Zeitung, 6 March 1928

Part IV

USSR

28

The Czarist Émigrés
(1926)

Long before we thought of visiting the new Russia, the old one came to us. The émigrés brought with them the wild aroma of their homeland, of dispossession, of blood and poverty, of their singular romantic destiny. It suited our clichéd European notions of Russians that they had experienced such things, that they found themselves expelled from their warm hearths, were aimless wanderers through the world, were derailed. We were armed with the old literary formula reflexively applied for every transgression and excess: "the Russian soul". Europe was familiar with music-hall Cossacks, the operatic excesses of Russian peasant weddings, Russian singers and their balalaikas. It never understood (not even after the Russians turned up on our doorstep) how French *romanciers*—the most conservative in the world—and sentimental Dostoyevsky readers had deformed the Russian to a kitschy figure compounded of divinity and bestiality, alcohol and philosophy, samovar cosiness and the barren steppes of Asia. As for the Russian woman! A kind of human animal endowed with remorse and adulterous passion, wasteful and rebellious, a writer's wife and a bomb-maker. The longer the emigration went on, the more our Russians resembled the notion we had of them. They flattered us by assimilating themselves to it. Their feeling of playing a part maybe soothed their misery. They bore it more easily once it was appreciated as literature. The Russian count as Paris cabbie takes his fares straight into a storybook. His fate itself may be ghastly. But it is at least literary.

The anonymous life of the émigrés became a public production. And then they began to make an exhibition of themselves. Hundreds of them founded theatres, choirs, dance groups, balalaika orchestras. For two years they were all new, authentic, stupefying. After a while they became boring and redundant. They lost their connection to their native soil. They grew ever further away from Russia—and Russia from them. Europe had heard of Meyerhold— meanwhile they were still retailing Stanislavsky. The "blue birds" started to sing in French, English and German. Finally they flew to America and started to moult.

The émigrés saw themselves as the only rightful representatives of Russia. What grew to significance in Russia following the Revolution was decried as "un-Russian" or "Jewish" or "cosmo- politan". Europe had long since got used to seeing Lenin as a representative of Russia. The émigrés were back with Nicholas II. They clung to the past with moving fealty, but they transgressed against history. And they took away from their own tragedy as well.

Oh, but they had to live. That's why they appeared in staged Cossack gallops in the Paris Hippodrome with alien horses, dressed with crooked Turkish scimitars that they bought at the fair in Clignancourt, took empty bandoliers and blunt daggers out in Montmartre, stuffed catskin bearskins on their heads and inspired awe as Don chieftains outside the doors of tacky establishments, even if they had been born in Volhynia. Some erased their trails with stateless Nansen passports and became archdukes. No one cared anyway. They were all equally good at plucking their home- sickness and their melancholy on their balalaikas, putting on red morocco leather boots with silver spurs and spinning round on one heel kicking up their legs. I saw a duchess performing a Russian wedding in a Parisian *variété*. She was the blushing bride;

night-watchmen from the Rue Pigalle, dressed as boyars, stood either side, ranked like flowerpots; a cardboard cathedral sparkled in the background; from it emerged the priest with a candy-floss beard; glass jewels shone in the Russian sun, which emerged from a spotlight; and the band dribbled the song of the Volga into the hearts of the audience from pizzicato violins. The other noble-women were played by waitresses in various bars, notepads hung from Tula silver chains on their aprons. Their heads sat proudly atop their necks, models of rigid émigré tragedy.

Others, broken, sat slumped on the benches of the Tuileries, the Jardins du Luxembourg, the Viennese Prater, the Berlin Tiergarten, the banks of the Danube in Budapest, and the cafés of Constantinople. They were in touch with the reactionaries of their respective host nations. They sat there and mourned their fallen sons and daughters, their missing wives—but also the gold watch, a present from Alexander III. Many had left Russia because they couldn't stand "the wretchedness of the country" any more. I know Russian Jews expropriated only a few years before by Denikin and Petljura, who now hate nothing in the world so much as Trotsky, who hasn't lifted a finger to hurt them. They want the return of their false baptismal certificate with which they once humbly, unworthily sneaked their way into the great forbidden Russian cities.

In the little hotel in the Quartier Latin where I stayed, lived one of the well-known Russian "counts", along with his father, wife, children and a "bonne". The old count was still the genuine arti-cle. He heated his soup on a spirit burner, and even though I knew him to be a leading anti-Semite and a figure in the exploitation of the peasantry, there was still something moving about him. He would crawl shivering through the damp evenings of autumn, a symbol, no longer a human being, a leaf, dissevered from the tree of life. But his son, brought up abroad, elegantly clad by Parisian tailors, kept by better-off noblemen—the difference! In the telephone exchange he conferred with former life guards, sent birthday greetings to genuine and fake Romanovs, and left kitschy pink *billets-doux* in the mailboxes of ladies staying in the hotel. He drove to czarist congresses, and he lived like a little émigré god in France. Soothsayers, priests, fortune tellers and theosophists beat a path to his door, all those who knew what the future held for Russia, namely the return of Catherine the Great and the troika, bear-hunts and *katorga*, Rasputin and the serf system.

They all lost their way. They lost their Russianness and their nobility. And because that was all they had ever been—Russian noblemen—they lost everything. They fell out of the bottom of their own tragedy. The great drama was left without heroes. History bitterly and implacably took its course. Our eyes grew tired of watching a misery they had revelled in. We stood before the last of them, the ones that couldn't understand their own catastrophe, we knew more about them than they could tell us, and arm in arm with Time, at once cruel and sad, we left these lost souls behind.

Frankfurter Zeitung, 14 September 1926

29

The Border at Niegoreloye
(1926)

T he border at Niegoreloye is a large wood-panelled room we all have to pass through. Kindly porters have fetched our luggage off the train. The night is very dark, it's cold, and it's raining. That's why the porters seemed so kindly. With their white aprons and their strong arms, they came to our aid, when we visitors encountered the frontier. An authorized official had taken my passport off me in the train, leaving me with no identity. So, myself and not myself, I crossed the frontier. I might have been mixed up with any other traveller. Later, though, it transpired that the Russian customs inspectors were incapable of any confusion. More intelligent than their colleagues in the service of other nations, they already knew the purpose of my visit.

We were expected. Warm yellow electric lights had been lit in the wood-panelled hall. At the desk where the chief inspector sat, there burned—like a friendly greeting from other times—a smiling oil-lamp. The clock on the wall showed the Eastern European time. The travellers, in their eagerness to get where they were going, promptly adjusted their watches. It wasn't ten any more, it was eleven. Our train was leaving at midnight.

We were few, but our suitcases were many. Most of them belonged to a diplomat. According to international law, these remained untouched. As virginal as they had been when they left, they would also have to arrive. They contained so-called secrets of state. That didn't mean that careful note couldn't be made of each and every one of them. It took a long time. The most efficient inspectors had their hands full with the diplomat. And in the meantime, Eastern European time ticked on.

Outside, in the damp black night, the Russian train was being made ready. Russian locomotives don't whistle, they howl like ship's sirens, wide, cheerful and oceanic. Looking through the window and hearing the locomotive, you feel you are by the sea. The hall starts to feel cosy. Suitcases throw open their lids and spread out, as though they felt the heat. Wooden toys clamber out of the stout trunks of a merchant from Tehran, snakes and chickens and rocking horses. Little skipjacks rock from side to side on their lead-weighted bellies. Their bright ridiculous faces, garishly lit by the oil lamp, and darkened by the swift shadows of hands, come to life, change their expressions, laugh, grin and cry. The toys climb up on a set of kitchen scales, are weighed, tumble down onto the desk again, and wrap themselves in rustling crepe paper. The suitcase of a young, pretty and rather desperate woman yields lengths of coloured silk, pieces of a cut-up rainbow. There follows wool which breathes, expands, consciously inflates after so many days of an airless constricted existence. Slender grey shoes slip out of the newspaper designed to keep them hidden, page four of *Le Matin*. Gloves with ornamented cuffs climb out of a little coffin of cardboard. Underwear, handkerchiefs, evening gowns float up, all barely of a size to dress the hand of an inspector. All the playful accoutrements of a rich world, all the satiny, polished little *riens* lie there strange and trebly useless in this hard brown nocturnal hall, under the heavy oak beams, under the admonitory posters with jagged letters like sharpened hatchets, in the aroma of resin, leather and petrol. There are the trim and corpulent bottles of emerald green and amber yellow liquids, leather manicure sets open their wings like holy shrines, little ladies' slippers sashay across the desk.

Never have I witnessed such a detailed inspection, not even in the years immediately after the War, in the golden age of inspectors. It seems this isn't a border between one country and another, but one between one world and another. The proletarian customs inspector—the most expert in the world: how often he has had to conceal something himself and get away with it!—examines what are citizens of neutral and allied states, but people of an enemy class. They are traders and specialists, ambassadors of capital. They come to Russia, called by the state, but at war with the proletariat. The official knows that these merchants are here to sow order forms in the shops which will flower into wonderful, expensive, unaffordable wares. He checks first the faces and then the suitcases. He can tell the homecomers, despite their new Polish, Serbian or Persian passports.

Late at night, the travellers are still standing in the train corridor unable to get over the customs inspection. They tell each other everything, what they brought, what they paid, what they smuggled. Material there for long Russian winter evenings. Their grandchildren will have to listen to their stories.

The grandchildren will listen, and the strange, confusing aspect of our time will loom before them, time at its own frontiers, time with its perplexed children, with Red customs officials and White travellers, false Persians, Red Army types in long sand-coloured greatcoats, their hems brushing the ground, the damp night at Niegoreloye, the loud wheezing of heavily laden porters. No question, this frontier has a historic dimension. I feel it the moment the siren wails loud and hoarse, and we bob out into the dark, calm expanse ahead.

Frankfurter Zeitung, 21 September 1926

30

Down the Volga to Astrakhan
(1926)

The Volga steamer that goes from Nizhny Novgorod to Astrakhan lies at anchor white and festive, like a Sunday. A man shakes a small, surprisingly noisy bell. The porters come running through the wooden departure hall, dressed only in track suit bottoms and a leather carrying strap. They look like so many wrestlers. Hundreds of them stand by the counter. It's nine o'clock on a bright morning. A happy wind is blowing. It feels as if a circus has just put up its tents outside the town.

The Volga steamer bears the name of a famous hero of the Revolution and has four classes of passenger. In the first are the new citizens of Russia, the NEP-men on their way to holidays in the Caucasus and the Crimean peninsula. They eat in the dining room, in the scrawny shade of a palm tree, facing the portrait of the famous hero of the Revolution, which is nailed up over the door. The young daughters of the comrades play on the harsh piano. It sounds like metal spoons being struck on glasses of tea. Their fathers play cards and complain about the government. A few of their mothers manifest a predilection for orange scarves. The waiter is not class-conscious. He was already a waiter back in the days when the steamers were named for archdukes. A tip brings so much submissiveness into his face, you forget the Revolution.

Fourth class is in the belly of the ship. Those passengers lug heavy bundles, rickety baskets, musical instruments and agricultural equipment. All nations, those on the Volga and beyond, are represented among them: Chuvaish, Chuvans, gypsies, Jews, Germans, Poles, Russians, Kazakhs, Kirghiz. There are Catholics here, Russian Orthodox, Muslims, Tibetans, heathens, Protestants. Here are old people, fathers, mothers, girls, infants. Here are small-farm workers, poor artisans, wandering musicians, blind buccaneers, travelling merchants, half-grown shoe-shine boys, and homeless children, so-called *bezprizorniy* who live off wretchedness and fresh air. They all sleep in wooden drawers, two storeys one above the other. They eat pumpkins, hunt for lice in the children's hair, still their infants, wash nappies, brew tea, and play the balalaika and the mouth organ.

By day this narrow space is shamefully noisy and unfit for occupation. At night, though, a kind of respect blows through it. That's how holy poverty looks sleeping. All the faces have on them the real pathos of naïveté. All the faces look like open gates through which one can see into clear white souls. Confused hands try to chase away the painful lights like so many pesky flies. Men bury their faces in the hair of their wives, farmers hug their flails, children their tawdry dolls. The lamps swing in time to the stamping engines. Red-cheeked girls smilingly show their white, strong teeth. A great peace is over the poor world, and man—asleep, anyway—suggests he is a thoroughly peace-loving creature.

But the separation on the Volga steamer is not the simple separation of rich and poor. Among the fourth-class passengers are rich farmers, among the first-class passengers are traders who aren't invariably rich. The Russian farmer prefers fourth. It's cheaper and that's not all. A farmer feels more at home there. The Revolution may have freed him of deference towards the master, but not yet of respect for the object. The farmer cannot tuck into his pumpkin with gusto in a restaurant with a bad piano. For a few months, everyone travelled in all different classes. Then they went their own ways, almost willingly.

"You see," an American said to me on the boat, "what has the Revolution achieved? The poor folks huddle in steerage, and the rich play cards on deck."

"But that's the only thing they can do without apprehension," I replied. "The poorest shoe-shine boy in fourth class has the confidence he could come up and be among us if he wanted. The rich NEP-men are afraid of precisely that. 'Up' and 'down' are not symbolic any more on this steamer, they are purely technical. Maybe they'll be symbolic again in the future."

"You reckon?" said the American.

The sky over the Volga is close and flat and painted with unmoving clouds. On either side, beyond the banks, you can see every single tree, every soaring bird, every grazing animal for miles and miles. A wood here has the effect of an artificial formation. Everything tends to spread out and to scatter. Villages, towns and peoples are far apart. Farms, huts, tents of nomadic people stand there, surrounded by isolation. The many tribes do not mix. Even the person who has settled somewhere remains on the move all his life. This earth gives the feeling of freedom that we ordinarily only get from air and water. If birds could walk here, they wouldn't bother flying. Man skims over the land as if it were sky, cheerful and aimless, a bird of the earth.

The river is like the land: wide, endlessly long (it is over fifteen hundred miles from Nizhny Novgorod to Astrakhan) and very slow. On its banks it takes a long time for the "Volga hills" to appear, little low cubes. Their bare rocky insides face the river. They are only there for the sake of variety, a playful caprice of God's created them. Behind them the flat land goes on for ever, pushing the horizon further and further back into the steppe.

It sends its great breath out over the hills and the river. You can taste the bitterness of infinity on your tongue. In sight of great hills and shoreless seas you feel threatened and lost. Facing the great plains, man is lost but somehow comforted. He may be little more than a blade of grass, but he won't go under: he is like a child waking up very early on a summer morning when everyone else is still asleep. You feel lost and at the same time privileged in the endless silence. When a fly buzzes, or a muffled pendulum gongs, it has the same effect of mingled sorrow and consolation as this endless plain.

We stop at villages built of wood and clay, roofed with straw and shingles. Sometimes the broad, motherly dome of a church sits in the middle of the huts, her children. Sometimes the church stands at the head of a long row of huts and has a thin, sharp, pointed tower like a four-sided French bayonet. It's a church under arms, leading a wandering village.

Kazan, the Tartar capital, stands before us. Colourful noisy tents throng the shore. Open windows beckon like glass flags. We hear the drumming of its droshkies. We see the green and golden evening shimmer of its cupolas.

A road leads from the harbour to Kazan. The road is a stream, it rained yesterday. In the town quiet pools. Leftovers of plaster occasionally stick up into the air. The street signs and shop names are mud-spattered and illegible. Doubly illegible, because they are partly written in an old Turkic-Tartar script. The Tartars prefer to sit outside their shops and tell passers-by of their wares. They are canny traders, as is their reputation. They wear black brush chin beards. Since the Revolution, illiteracy has fallen by twenty-five per cent. Now many of them can read and write. The bookshops stock Tartar publications, the paper boys sell Tartar newspapers. Tartar officials sit behind post office counters. One official told me the Tartars were the bravest people there are. "But they're mixed with Finns," I countered maliciously. The official was offended. With the exception of pub landlords and traders, everyone is happy with the government. The Tartar farmers sided now with the Reds, now with the Whites. Often they didn't understand what it was about. Today all the villages in Kazan province are politicized. Young people are members of various Komsomol organizations. As with most of the Muslim nationalities in Russia, religion is more a matter of habit than faith. The Revolution has disrupted a habit more than suppressed a need. The poor peasants here are happy as they are all over the Volga province. Having lost much, the rich farmers are as unhappy as they are everywhere else, as the Germans in Pokrovsk, or the farmers of Stalingrad and Saratov.

The Volga villages—with the exception of the German ones—supply the Party with its most enthusiastic young supporters. In the Volga districts, political enthusiasm comes more from the countryside than the urban proletariat. Many of the villages here were at a great remove from culture. The Chuvaish for instance are still secretly "heathen" today. They worship idols. For the naïve person grown up in a Volga village, communism is civilization. For the young Chuvaish the Red Army barracks in town is a palace, and the palace—into which he gains admission—is seven hundred heavens. Electricity, newspaper, wireless, book, ink, typewriter, cinema, theatre—all those things we find so wearisome, to the primitive person are refreshing and enlivening. All laid on by the Party. It not only put the masters in their places, it invented the telephone and the alphabet. It taught a man to be proud of his people, his smallness, even his poverty. Faced by the onrush of so many wonders, his instinctive peasant mistrust is vanquished. His critical sense is still a long way from being awakened. So he becomes a fanatic of this new faith. The "collectivist sense" that the peasant lacks he makes up for twice and threefold by simple ecstasy.

The towns on the Volga are the saddest I have ever seen. They remind me of the destroyed towns on the French front. The buildings burned in the Civil War; and then their ruins saw the White hunger galloping through the streets.

People died a hundred deaths, a thousand deaths. They ate cats, dogs, crows, rats and their own starving children. They bit themselves and drank the blood. They scratched the earth for fat earthworms and lumps of white chalk which looked to the eye like cheese. Two hours after they had eaten they died in torments. How could these towns even be alive still! How could people haggle and carry suitcases and sell apples and have children! Already a generation is growing up that does not know the Terror, already there are scaffoldings, with carpenters and masons busily building anew.

I am not surprised that these towns are only beautiful from a distance or from above; that in Samara a goat refused to let me enter my hotel; that a downpour drenched me in my room in Stalingrad; that the napkins are coloured packing paper. If only one could walk over the nice roofs instead of the bumpy cobbles.

In all of the Volga towns you come across the same things: the traders are unhappy, the workers are hopeful, but tired, the waiters respectful and unreliable, the porters humble, the shoeshine boys submissive. And everywhere young people are revolutionary—half the middle-class youth is enrolled in pioneer and Komsomol organizations.

People respond to the way I dress: if I put on a pair of top-boots and go without a tie, life suddenly becomes incredibly cheap. Fruit costs a few kopecks, a ride in a droshky half a rouble. I am taken for a foreign political refugee residing in Russia and they call me "comrade". The waiters have proletarian consciousness and expect no tip, the shoeshine boys are happy with ten kopecks, the traders are happy with their lot, and in the post office the peasants ask me to address a letter for them, "with tidy writing". But how expensive the world becomes when I put on a tie! I am addressed as "Grashdanin" (citizen) or sometimes, shyly, "Gospodin" (sir). The German beggars address me as "Herr Landsmann" (compatriot). The traders start to complain about the taxes. The conductor expects a rouble. The waiter in the dining car tells me he studied at trade school and is "a bit of an intellectual". He proves it by charging me an extra twenty kopecks. An anti-Semite grumbles that the only people who did well out of the Revolution are the

Jews. They were even allowed to live in Moscow now. He tells me he was an officer in the war, and had been taken prisoner in Magdeburg. A NEP-man threatens me: "Don't think you'll be able to see everything that goes on here."

And it seems to me that I see just as much and just as little in Russia as I do anywhere else. I was never so generously, naturally invited by strangers as here. I am allowed to go into offices, law-courts, hospitals, schools, barracks, police stations, prisons, to police commanders and university professors. The middle classes are more loudly and forthrightly critical than is agreeable for a stranger. I can talk to Red Army privates and commanders in pubs about war, pacifism, literature and weaponry. In other countries this is more dangerous. The secret police are probably so discreet that I am not even aware of them.

THE FAMOUS BARGE HAULERS on the Volga still go singing their famous song. In the Russian cabarets of the West, the "Burlaki" are portrayed with purple lighting and pizzicato violins. But the real Burlaki are sadder than their representatives can have any idea. Even though they are so burdened with traditional romance, their song slips deep and painfully into the hearer.

They may well be the strongest men alive. Every one of them can carry two hundred and forty kilogrammes on his back, snatch a hundred kilos off the ground, crush a nut between index and middle fingers, balance an oar on two fingers, eat three pumpkins in three-quarters of an hour. They look like bronze statues covered with human skin and given a carrying strap. They are relatively well paid, between four and six roubles. They are strong, healthy, they live on the river, free. But I have never seen them laugh. They have no capacity for joy. They drink. Alcohol does for these giants. Ever since freight has been carried on the Volga the strongest porters live here, and they all drink. Today more than 100 steamers and 1200 barges sail on the Volga, a total tonnage of almost 2 million.

But the haulers still do the work of mechanical cranes just as they did two hundred years ago.

Their song doesn't come from their throats, but from the unknown depths of their hearts where destiny and song are woven together. They sing like people sentenced to death. They sing like prisoners on the galleys. Never will a singer be free of his towing rope, or from alcohol. Work is a blessing! A man is a crane!

It's rare to hear a whole song, only the odd verse, or a few bars. Music is a mechanical support, it works like a lever. There are songs you sing when you pull on a rope together, when you lift, when you unload, when you lower. The words are ancient and primitive. I have heard different words sung to the same tunes. Some of them are about a hard life, an easy death, a thousand pud, and girls and love. As soon as the load is lifted onto your back, the song is over. Then man is a crane.

I can't go back to the glass piano and the card games. I leave the steamer. I am sitting on a tiny boat. Two *burlaki* beside me sleep gently on hawsers. In four or five days we will be in Astrakhan. The captain has sent his wife to bed. He is his own crew. Now he is preparing his shashlik. I expect it will be fatty and gristly, and I will have to share it with him.

Before I got off, the American drew a big arc with his index finger, pointing at the chalky, clayey soil and the sandy banks, and said:

"See all the raw materials lying here unused! What a beach this would be for invalids and people needing a rest! That sand! If only all this whole Volga were in some civilized part of the world!"

"If it was in some civilized part of the world, there would be factory chimneys, nippy motor boats, black cranes swinging back and forth, people would fall ill so that they could recover two miles away in the sand, and it wouldn't be a desert. At a certain, hygienically determined distance from the cranes, there would be restaurants and cafés, with ozone terraces. Bands would play the song of the Volga, and there would be a dapper Volga Charleston, with words by Arthur Rebner and Fritz Grünbaum ... "

"Ah, Charleston," cried my friend, and he cheered up.

Frankfurter Zeitung, 5 October 1926

31

The Wonders of Astrakhan
(1926)

In Astrakhan people fish and deal in caviar. The smells of these activities are spread throughout the town. Whoever isn't obliged to go to Astrakhan is advised to give it a miss. Whoever has come to Astrakhan will not stay there for very long. Among the specialities of this town are the famed Astrakhan furs: the lambskin hats, the silver-grey "Persian fur". The furriers are kept busy. In summer and winter alike (winters are warm here too) Russians, Kalmucks and Kirghiz all wear fur.

I am told that before the Revolution rich people used to live in Astrakhan. I am shown their houses, though many were destroyed in the Civil War. From their ruins you can tell they were boastful and had no taste. Of all the qualities of a building, boastfulness survives longest, the least brick thumps itself on the chest. The builders have fled, they are living abroad. It stands to reason they will have dealt in caviar. But what possessed them to live here where (black, blue, white) caviar grows, and where the fishes stink so mercilessly?

In Astrakhan there is a little park with a pavilion in the middle and a rotunda in the corner. In the evening you pay a small fee and you go in the park and sniff the fish. It is dark, so you picture them dangling from the trees. There are cinema performances in the open air, and primitive cabaret likewise. The bands play cheerful tunes from old times. People drink beer and eat cheap pink langoustines. Not one hour passes in which one doesn't pine for Baku. Unfortunately, the boat there goes only three times a week.

In order to lend plausibility to my dreams of the steamer, I go down to the harbour. No. 18 is the quay for the boat to Baku. The day after tomorrow.—My Lord, how remote is that! Kalmucks row, Kirghiz lead their camels on halters into town, caviar sellers shout in their offices, clueless peasants sleep out, two days and two nights, waiting for the boat, gypsies play cards. Because it is so evident that the steamship isn't coming, the mood in the harbour is sadder than in town. To get a faint sense of departure I treat myself to a droshky ride. The seats are narrow and backless, perilous, no roof, and the horses are in white Ku Klux Klan robes against the dust—as if they were going to a three-day event. The cabbies speak hardly any Russian, and hate the cobbles. They go down sandy streets, seeing as the horse is dressed for it. The passenger, having got on in a dark suit, gets off in a silver one. If I had set off in a white one, it would be dove-grey now. To be dressed for Astrakhan means wearing long hooded dust coats, like the horses. In the dimly illuminated night you can see ghosts being driven around by ghostly horses.

And for all that, Astrakhan has a technical college, libraries, clubs and theatres. Ice cream under a swaying arc lamp, fruit and marzipan behind bridal gauze. I pray for an end to the dust plague. The next day God sent a cloudburst. The ceiling of my hotel room, pampered by so much dust, wind and drought, promptly fell to the floor with shock. I hadn't asked for as much rain as all that. It thundered and lightened. The streets could not be made out. The droshkies groaned along, up to their axles in mud, the spokes dropped soft, grey, heavy clumps of it. The ghosts threw back their hoods and put up familiar human gear. Two couldn't pass each other on the cobbled main street. One had to turn round and go back at least twenty feet to let the other pass. You triple-jumped to cross the street. I was lucky in that everything I needed was on one block: hotel, writing paper, post office, and café.

In those days in Astrakhan the most important institution was the café. It was run by a Polish family brought here from Częstochowa by an implacable fate. I had to tell the women all about what they were wearing in Warsaw. I showed extensive knowledge of Polish politics. Doubts people in Astrakhan had about a war involving Poland, Russia and Germany I was able to allay at length. When I am in Astrakhan I am a witty conversationalist.

Without this café, I would have been unable to work, the most important means of production being coffee. There is no role for flies. And yet there they were, morning, noon and night. It is flies not fishes that make up ninety-eight per cent of the fauna of Astrakhan. They are perfectly useless, not a trading commodity, no one lives off them, they live off everyone. Thick black swarms of them sit on dishes, sugar, windows, china plates, leftovers, on bushes and trees, on dung heaps and excreta, and even on clean tablecloths where a human eye discerns nothing of nutritional value. A spilled drop of soup, long since absorbed into the cloth, these flies are capable of eating molecule by molecule, as though with a spoon. On the white tunics that most men here wear sit thousands of flies. Secure and contemplative, they don't fly up when their host moves, they are capable of sitting for hours at a time on his shoulders. The flies of Astrakhan are nerveless, they have the tranquillity of great mammals, like cats, or their enemies from the insect world, the spiders … I am surprised and sad that these intelligent and humane creatures do not come to Astrakhan in numbers where they could be of great benefit to the human race. I have eight garden-spiders in my room, quiet, clever animals, friendly associates of my sleepless nights. By day they sleep in their apartments. At dusk they move into position—two, the most prominent and gifted, to the proximity of the light. Long and patiently they watch the clueless flies, with their fine, hair-thin legs they clamber up ropes spun from nothing and spittle, carry out repairs and stay on the alert, surround their quarry on wide, wide detours, deftly make themselves fast to grains of sand on the wall, work hard and cleverly—but how poorly they are recompensed. A thousand flies buzz about my room, I wish I had twenty thousand poisonous spiders, a whole army of them! If I stay longer in Astrakhan, I would breed them and show them more attention than caviar.

But the people of Astrakhan are only interested in caviar. They are oblivious to the flies. They watch these murderous insects gnaw at their meat, their bread, their fruit, and they don't raise a finger. Yes, the flies stroll about on their beards, their noses and foreheads, and the people talk and laugh. In the café, they have given up the fight against the flies, they don't even bother to shut the glass vitrine, they let them gorge themselves on sugar and chocolate, they veritably spoil them. Fly-paper, invented by an American, the thing I most detest among all civilization's blessings, strikes me as a work of noble idealism when I am in Astrakhan. But the whole of Astrakhan has not one scrap of that precious yellow stuff. I ask them in the café: "Why don't you have any fly-paper?" They answer evasively and say: "Oh, if only you'd been in Astrakhan before the war, even a couple of months before!" The landlord says it, and the trader. They lend passive support to the reactionary flies. One day these little beasts will eat up the whole of Astrakhan, fishes and caviar and all.

I prefer the beggars to the flies of Astrakhan, more numerous here than anywhere else. They wander slowly through the streets, wailing or singing at the tops of their voices, crying their woes as though following their own corpse, pouring into every beer hall. I give them a kopeck—and on that kopeck they manage to live! Of all the wonders of Astrakhan they are really the most astonishing ...

Frankfurter Zeitung, 12 October 1926

32

Saint Petroleum

(1926)

There is an electric railway from Baku to Sabunchi, where vast quantities of petroleum are extracted. It wasn't built till last year, and is still unfinished. (The trams in Baku are also the work of the Soviet government.) The people are proud of this railway. The Soviet government views it as a local, but highly effective propaganda success. It seems likely that earlier enterprises extracted petroleum more cheaply and used it more efficiently than the present nationalized enterprise. But it is also true that neither the Nobels nor the Rothschilds ever built a tramline for their workforce. All of them were made to cover great distances on foot, in dog-carts, or on primitive farm wagons. Now a spacious, hygienic, modern train leaves Baku every half hour. The Western European is not surprised to see it. But to a Soviet citizen, this railway is not only an acclaimed, long-missed conveyance; it is almost, it is in fact, a symbol. It is the only railway of its kind in the whole of Russia. What to us would be an unsurprising technical innovation in this corner of Eurasia carries political weight. The line preserves and encourages the optimism of the oil workers, many of whom earn comparatively high wages (up to three hundred roubles a month), who have an old revolutionary tradition, and are therefore predisposed to believe in the new state. So rails and carriages, bricks and cement, are capable of

political and historical significance. The old entrepreneurs seem
not to have considered this as a possibility.

Long before the train moves off the carriages are all full. It's hot,
and a slothful wind seems for once to have taken the place of the
prevailing breeze. The sun pierces the windows and heats up walls,
floor and ceiling. All the passengers are complaining about the
heat—a welcome pretext for conversation. I see Turkish workers
with the Red Flag, many of them with Party badges—beside them
Turkish women, ritually covered features, an old sheikh for whom
people move aside, maybe not reverently but with that degree of
tolerance that is not yet a matter of course, and resembles politeness. An Armenian priest is reading a book, a holy book I had
thought; but not at all, it is one of the many brochures produced
from the new camp. A vendor comes by with Oriental sweets,
halvah and baklava, sticky, sugar-powdered, sometimes garish and
yet bland things, chewing gum you gulp down if you can get it clear
of your teeth. The homeless children or *bezprizorniy* hunker down
on the steps, wangle their way through the feet of the passengers,
are picked up, thrown out, and creep miraculously back in through
cracks and openings. There are a lot of proles and semi-proles—all
drawn by petroleum—it looks menacing, but it's harmless and
hungry. Many people have stunningly beautiful eyes, shining and
still haunted. I think of the heavy, tired blink of the Armenian, the
veiled, tragic expression of Jewish […] Turko-Tartars, the large
moist pupils of the Muslim woman looking out between dense
cloth wrappings like an animal between stout bars. The conductor
begs to be let through. He wears a yellow tunic with tasteful
badges, and looks like a British conductor in the colonies. This is
a modern, technical Russia with American ambitions. Not a real
Russia any more.

These towers suddenly popping up, black, dense, iron—these
towers are no longer Russia. They are drilling towers, triumphs,
symbols and revelations of the great power called petroleum;

"nyeft" in Russian. The word expresses all the sweating fluidity of the substance. A historical sound and a historical sight. An atmosphere of capital, adventure, sensation and novelty. The greatest colonial power looks to these towers, and the greatest continental power holds on to them. This region alone produces at least half a million tonnes a day, the Caucasian earth is very liberal. Thousands of square miles are still unexplored and promising, volcanoes that issue fire signals every few months, betraying subterranean billions. (How barren and petty by comparison is the Galician soil of Drohobycz and Boryslav!) Give us money, money, money! chant the towers. We are ten thousand, twenty thousand—we want to be a hundred thousand, we want to be millions!

Outside Sabunchi's little station is a blue-green lake, and beyond it a wild, shambolic, steep, treacherous, shitty, dusty path. It leads to the wells and into the town, up a small hill, with a church on its peak, lost, eccentric, puzzled, a feeble competitor to the towers, all alone among twenty thousand foes, cheek by jowl with the Soviet authorities. Left and right of the lake wait endless swarms of dusty droshkies. The coachmen stand upright like Roman charioteers, all of them shouting for custom. Around Sabunchi there are some quiet, distinguished dachas, or summerhouses. Sometimes—not often—a few passengers turn up to go out to the dachas. But there are a hundred times more "phaetons". All the coachmen call out "Barin!" (Sir!) at once. Each one thinks twenty times a day the fare will choose him, and twenty times he is disappointed, and a thousand times he calls out. Here there are no probabilities, here a profession is a lottery. That's what people are like: for the sake of tiny odds they will waste an entire day. Coachmen are gamblers.

The traders outside their sad Oriental booths shout themselves hoarse. Their quiet Oriental souls are agitated. Petroleum changes human nature. It ignites people even before it has left the ground. Here its aspect is more Asiatic than Russian. This is the gold-rush town from an American movie.

On the left is the market place. Extremely, preternaturally big green pumpkins litter the ground with their ovals and spheres. Fruits like a race of giants, the succulent diet of the people. Who eats so many pumpkins? More than twenty thousand workers live in Sabunchi; here are at least three times that number of pumpkins. These fruits of a lavish nature almost completely eclipse the grapes, the dates, the figs, the pears. There are a hundred stalls selling fruit, bread, meat, fat pigs, big, black-spotted, heavy, but nimble as dogs, pigs in a hurry: another whim of this southern nature. On the right, on the hilly ground are dwellings, sad, naked, reddish: they look flayed. The corridors are deep and black, the flats are open, the rooms give off a dull warmth, the dense aroma of a constricted life that is not unlike the smell of death. All round no horizon, only towers, towers, towers, black, cross-hatched, clustered together— as though they couldn't stand unaided. They are so numerous and frail that they flicker and move. You turn away, oppressed by their grotesque numbers. When you turn back, it's as though there were somehow more of them, they press and spawn and make more, they will eat up the big marketplace, the giant pumpkins, the mouldy, diseased houses.

The houses are temporary. The workers who live in them today will drift off to the settlements in a couple of years. For model working settlements are under construction in Azerbaijan. I go to look at one, not quite finished, already two-thirds inhabited. It's called "Stenka Razin" after the Russian folk hero, the first farmer revolutionary who stole from the rich and gave to the poor, the lord of the Volga delta and the Caspian Sea, still revered today by the people with a tender affection that is far removed from hero-worship.

A deep gorge cuts through a mountain; people tell me it opens onto the sea. Stenka Razin dug it. Here he hid his stolen goods, from here he could run away. In the workers' settlement there will be a monument to him, in the middle of a lawn: he never dreamed it would come to that. An alien doctrine adopted him after the fact. It would have struck him as odd. But it's well-intentioned, and maybe he'd have come round to it. There is a playground for children, a club, a theatre, a cinema, a library. The buildings are ground level. Later they will grow up to be bungalows, because that's the cheapest way. Moscow architects have devised more than a score of styles. Animatedness, difference, variety are the aim; no uniformity.

Only two years ago the earth was still bald, hostile, swampy, stiff. It breathed out death. The fact that it is now alive confirms the wonder-working force of socialism. How modest they are. In our capitalist Ruhrgebiet, which I visited in spring, they use the same means to turn the workers into little bourgeois. Here, they turn them into revolutionaries. Here as there: tin baths, electric sockets, space for a flowerpot, functional and practical furniture screwed to the floor, waxed boards you don't have to scrub, a quiet gleam, a short sofa. How much that is already! And how little! The needs of the proletariat remain modest, whether he rules or is ruled. I think it's to do with labour. There it's coalmines, here the drilling towers. What a delight to man is a drill! How much more do you require of life if you spend eight hours, or six, or four, drilling for petroleum, for Saint Petroleum!?

Oh, I fear work is only a blessing because it stands in for joy.

Written in October 1926 for the Russian series,
but never printed

Part V

Albania

33

A Meeting with President Ahmed Zogu

(1927)

On Saturday at five in the afternoon, I go to meet the president of the Republic of Albania.* His house is under military guard. The sentries salute. His aide is waiting in the anteroom. He is young, slender, a major; pleasant, briefed and ready to talk about the weather, the Albanian landscape and the perils of malaria; what you call an aide.

In the president's room there is a portly, clever, older gentleman, who is the foreign secretary. He functions as interpreter and minder. The president wears the uniform of a general. Following some rule that insists a head of state needs a desk, Ahmed Zogu steps out from behind his. Greetings are exchanged. I am engulfed by an armchair. The president tells the minister in Albanian that he is happy to welcome the representative of a great German newspaper to his country; the great German people can be assured

---

* The recipient here of J.R.'s dusty cool had himself made king the following year (King Zog I), remained in power until 1938, and finally died in exile in France in 1961. He is buried in the Cimetière Parisien de Thiais, where Roth lies too. He was the object of some six hundred blood feuds—vendettas—and survived fifty-five assassination attempts.

of the sympathies of the little Albanian people. The minister relays it to me, in French. The president permits me to travel the length and breadth of Albania free and unhindered, and with the support of the state. The minister repeats it in French. A bow. Another bow. Another. At this point, Ahmed Zogu switches to German. (He once served in Austria.) Had I been in Albania long. How long I anticipated staying. When and where I proposed to go. He desired nothing from reporters but the truth. The truth, I replied, was relative. Something that was true to one person could be a falsehood to another. Certainly, German reporters were obsessed with the need for truthfulness.

I had no particular questions for him—I could answer them all for myself. Interviews are an alibi for a journalist's lack of ideas.

I extricate myself from the armchair. Smiles wreathe three faces. A bow. Another bow. Another. Sentries. Salutes.

As far as the ceremonial of the audience goes, the Albanian version is indistinguishable in point of ritual, custom and awkwardness from those of any other country. Ahmed Zogu is younger than most European presidents; he is a tad over thirty. He has had a richer, more dramatic life than most Europeans his age. He has dead enemies on his conscience and living ones at large in his country. This last, again, is common to statesmen the world over; the former—more the dead enemies part than the conscience—is an Oriental speciality. Ahmed Zogu looks harmless enough, tall, as representative as he needs to be, and oddly, blond. The blondness overlies the Oriental features like a mistake. The posture he adopts when giving audiences is more the result of caution than any personal confidence. The sparseness of his speech, the slowness of his tongue, the empty politeness of his questions, all are the expression of an insufficiently practised and therefore all the more rigidly adhered-to diplomacy. He strives—for no good reason—for a crown-prince-like banality.

His military abilities are said to be small. In the Great War he did not, contrary to the claims of a swiftly circulated legend, enter Durazzo at the head of a column of Albanian troops. But in this country where every tenth peasant is a military genius, and every second a dead shot with a rifle, it is difficult to shine through military gifts. He is said to be a ruthless dictator. But in Albania, where every warlord has aspirations to be a dictator, every landowner his vassal, and anyone who can read and write his secretary, there is probably no other dictatorship going than the ruthless kind. Ahmed seems if anything less dictatorial than the people around him, who are more experienced, clever, and ruthless than he is, and many of whom have undergone a thorough education in these qualities under the Turks. Of all the qualities that underpin rather than grace dictatorship, the president of the Republic of Albania has perhaps only worry for the future of his country—understandably, in a country where a man doesn't even have to be dictator to fear a casual bullet. Further, Ahmed has enjoyed lavish hospitality from the South Slavs, having "conquered" Albania with the help of South Slav bands before shortly afterwards concluding the familiar pact with Italy. But for more than 800 years most of the influential men in the Balkans have not refused money, especially when offered by two opposing sides—and why should Ahmed be the exception here? The selfless friendship of the South Slavs has not yet been proved, in any case. But even if I (rightly) question the selfless patriotism of Ahmed, in many points the selfish ambition of the president tallies with the true needs of his country, which, faced with the choice between putting itself in the care of a more cultivated country or one still fighting with its unresolved internal difficulties, chooses the former. Further, the president is accused of plastering his image on walls, stamps and coins everywhere. But even in more developed nations, the widely circulated likeness is still seen as the best means of establishing oneself in the mostly brief and ungrateful consciousness of an electorate.

In any case, it is impossible to judge the circumstances of an

Oriental state, whose history is oppression, whose ethics are corruption, and whose culture is a mixture of native bucolic and archaic-romantic naïveté and the recent importation of intrigue, by the criteria of a Western democracy. If one suddenly found oneself back in the Middle Ages, it would be similarly fatuous to be exercised about the burning of witches.

One should try to judge Ahmed with an unprejudiced eye as an expression of his surroundings. One should bear in mind that he is the scion of an Albanian noble family that was in power in the seventeenth century and before—and presumably not with democratic methods then. One should bear in mind that a parliament in Albania can only be convoked in one way, the way that it is presently convoked. It will be a "parliament in name only" for at least another twenty years. It is just as open to the influence of cliques, the will of the head of state as the South Slav *Skupština*, and just as powerless as the parliaments in Budapest or Ankara. One should bear in mind that the rivals and enemies of Ahmed Zogu, some of whom I know personally, are no more Western than the man himself. Of the nine hundred and twenty Western-educated men who have left the country since Ahmed's accession, of the seven politicians who have fled to the South Slav Republic since 1925, of the twelve who since 1922 have lost their lives, I presume that none would want to exercise power in a different way than Ahmed Zogu—and I don't condemn them. Because in Oriental politics, and Albanian politics in particular, self-defence is a very broad concept, and one that plays almost the same role as reasons of state do in Western Europe. A long and laborious process of education needs to take place to make citizens out of shepherds, chieftains, warlords and religious fanatics.

Whether or not Ahmed Zogu is able or willing to take in hand this education is anyone's guess. Today even his ties to Italy make him nervous. He is no longer able to play off Italy and the South Slavs against each other. There is nothing he is more anxiously awaiting than an olive branch from the South Slavs. But the South Slavs are bitterly readying other men and methods. Italy is more concerned with protecting its own interests than Zogu's life. And so this young man, who has already had to suppress three revolts, in his well-cut general's uniform, with an immense allowance, in a by local standards palatial, by ours middle-class home, surrounded by a lifeguard whose loyalty is as relative as everything else in this country, advised by politicians whose cunning was sharpened and whose character dulled in Turkish service—this young man who might have led a carefree student existence in Paris, is stern and trembling, and awaiting a fourth revolt. Most of all, one doesn't take exception to the loss of life he is said to have been responsible for, so much as the sums of money he has obtained. But then again—if he didn't have them, then they would end up with others who would have deserved them even less; the small but lardy layer of alphabetical leeches, the Turkish scribes, the corrupt enablers of corruption.

Tomorrow may see Ahmed Zogu still in power, and the day after gone, and someone else in his place, who would be almost indistinguishable from him.

Frankfurter Zeitung, 29 May 1927

34

Arrival in Albania

(1927)

The sea is calm, the clouds hang in the sky as though nailed there, a ghostly boat skims across the placid surface towards the ship as though drawn on an invisible rope to collect me. There are only two of us disembarking here: a man hoping in this land of beards to sell Gillette razors, and myself.

Where terra firma begins there is a little wooden hut with a picture-book chimney from which the smoke goes straight up, as though drawn with a ruler. It's seven in the morning; wooded, green, bare, steel-blue mountains frame the horizon; cryptic larks flit about the shiny blue sky; the hut, like many attractions these days, has a guest-book; sitting over the book is a man in a black uniform, rolling himself a cigarette, and this is the Albanian border police. A master of the alphabet, but unused to writing, he sits there, whiling away the time of the new arrivals by painstaking scrutiny of their passports. A stooped Levantine chauffeur is kept waiting in the Ford he proposes to drive until the policeman has got to the end. I cut short his study by offering to set down my name for him.

Then, in a dense cloud of dust, amid the thunder of continually exploding tyres, thrown up and down by authentic Ford springs, I am taken along the road to Tirana. Each time a tyre needs changing, I get out, watch the dust settle and the scenery re-establish itself, mountains of a spectral violet, meadows of a twice-done green, sky of a dependable blue, a sky of cloth, a sky without wrinkles, a taut, carefully ironed arc. Workmen are repairing the road. There are always two hunched over together. Like children in kindergarten they collect little scoops of sand on their tiny shovels or in their bare hands, pour it into scars and potholes, sprinkle a few stones on top, wet the whole thing with water from a watering can and stamp it down with their bare feet. As soon as our Ford has passed, they can start the game again.

It's not long before we come to some soldiers. To see them march! In yellow-khaki columns, with steel helmets on their heads, rucksacks on their tired backs, burned by the sun, sweating and singing, they are marching for their new fatherland to Durazzo to exercise, escorted by an Albanian version of Mars with leather puttees, first lieutenant and spare uniform. On the juicy pastures a herd of cloudy white lambs is drifting about. Rams with ornamental curved horns, black oxen, a kind of beast of the underworld, the flocks of Hades. Either side there are telegraph wires, strung not on masts, but on crooked bare trees, which have been lopped and cropped. They once used to stand by the roadside, a home to birds, stopping places for evening winds; now they are redesignated as telegraph poles, fitted out with little white china panicles, and equipped to transmit journalistic reports—the twitterings of political sparrows—to Europe. On the left-hand side there is a set of rails, a narrow-gauge memento of the Austrians in the Great War, today given over to decay and the rusty tooth of time.

Finally a black-uniformed policeman, who can speak German, emerges from a white hut, takes our passports, and promises to have them left for us tomorrow morning in the police station at Tirana.

So here is Tirana, the capital city of Albania. On the right a mosque, on the left a rudimentary café terrace where guests bake and fezzes talk. The mosque turns out to be a barracks, soldiers with guns guard themselves. Every hotel room is taken, journalists have hurried here, and diplomats and parliamentarians, officers from England and Italy. Parliament is in session, Tirana is a burial-pit for sensation, imbroglios are on the street, the whole country is an apple of discord. Good citizens walk down the middle of the road, armed with muskets against sunstroke, heavy drum-revolvers stuck in wide, often doubled and tripled red sashes. Mules, laden with filled panniers, dawdle along the pavement, and wait outside shops like dogs while their masters make purchases. Here comes the majestic figure of the commander-in-chief of the Albanian army, Jemal Aranitas, mounted on a noble grey steed, little dark shoeshine boys fall over each other to get out of his way, a squire follows him, only a moment ago he was addressing the army, that's why their marching was so sorry, no state without a general, no general without a grey steed. Gold sparkles on his shoulders, he greets acquaintances at cafés with a casual wave.

A man turns up by the name of Nikola, who lets me a room. The bed has all four legs in petrol to keep the cockroaches at bay, the window is cracked at the bottom, and replaced at the top by a mos-quito net, my neighbour is a trumpeter. He is a member of the orchestra that plays outside the castle every afternoon.

A policeman with snow-white gloves stands in the middle of the road, in case of traffic.

Frankfurter Zeitung, 11 June 1927

Tirana, the Capital City
(1927)

The inhabitants of Tirana love music and flowers. You can see the men going around with roses in their mouths. They seem to use them as an extra buttonhole.

A section of the populace has devoted itself to brass instruments. Brass players—horns for the fatherland—have been recruited into the Albanian army. The soldiers' days begin with reveille and end with taps. Music keeps the swing in their stride.

The president has his very own personal band. The bandleader wears a pince-nez and hails from Trieste. The players are from Korça, in the melophile south, and from Czechoslovakia, which in the days when it was still the Kingdom of Bohemia used to supply the Army of the Dual Monarchy with the most sublime band sergeant majors. Every musician is paid fifteen napoleons a month. The acquisition and maintenance of the gorgeous uniforms— black with gold trimmings—is each individual's responsibility. On his cap every musician wears the familiar emblem of martial music: a golden lyre.

At seven in the morning, just as the soldiers are tooting and parping away, the musicians get up like so many larks, and rehearse passages of marches and overtures in the middle of the high street. The local inhabitants have petitioned the courts on six separate occasions to have the practice moved to a meadow outside the city.

But on six separate occasions they have forgotten to attach arguments to their petition. Nothing works without arguments.

Men who are neither in the army nor in the band are devoted to the mild plinking of the mandolin. They have for the most part been to America. There they had their teeth filled with gold, and bought themselves stringed instruments. They sing a song of bananas, to prove that they have seen the world, perhaps also as an expression of their painful longing for America, which they left on account of their painful longing for Tirana. Their hearts are still bobbing on the ocean wave, but their wares, which consist of combs, mirrors, letter paper, are in Tirana. A mandolin is a sheer inevitability.

They sit outside their shops in the sun for hours on end. It's very quiet. Musical predilections aside, Tirana is tranquil enough. When there is a lull in the blare, you hear the cocks crow, the hammers of the blacksmiths in the bazaar, and the regular summons to worship from the muezzin. The sun scorches down on the streets. The dust is baked in the heat, seeming to disintegrate into finer, thinner dust, dissolving in the atmosphere, disappearing into thin air, without anyone washing or sweeping the pavements. People say a young man is sent out by the authorities with a watering-can every morning, in the furtherance of hygiene, but no one has ever clapped eyes on him. But barracks are erected in the interests of progress. The dynamo that is to keep the electric lights going is too weak for so many bulbs. They come on at night, but they look like dying embers. They dangle on wires, like so many hanged glow-worms.

Bazaars have been knocked through, houses split and scalped, in order to make Tirana an up-to-date capital city. The half-buildings stand there, with black guts open. The residents exotically use the stoves as toilets, without taking off their pistols and rifles. Not for an instant is one safe from a vendetta.* Women in black and white

---

* Vendetta: a preoccupation presumably more of Roth's readership or editors than Roth himself, a blood-feud between two families or clans.

veils put one in mind of funeral processions or the KKK. They have shutters in front of their eyes at all times, they are walled in gauze and cloth. I would like to know what they get up to in their own homes. I am curious about them, they look like strange, illuminated, screened windows. The women are quiet as wild beasts and unresponsive as the dead. Are they crying? I can't see for sure. They talk to one another. But the sounds are trapped and their voices trickle thinly through the pores of the cloth like clear water through a choked and dirty sieve.

The veiled women, the hundreds of ownerless dogs led on the wind's leash, the fezzes on fat heads and turbans on bearded faces, the colour-postcard vendetta-artists with revolvers for bellies, and rifles for umbrellas—all these money-earning, business-conducting, official-bribing exotic philistines are in the majority and beyond time. There is nothing so arid as an ethnicity that has been dissected in the mausoleums of ethnology and in books and seminar rooms for thirty years, but is still paraded, as though it were in any sense alive. There is a parliament with a presidential suite and a bell, with order papers for interventions and a press balcony; there is a bank with sluggish Italian officials, with rates of exchange pinned up on boards like so many butterflies, with a loans manager. Already the owner of my hotel has taken to using his holster for keeping small change in, and on his sideboard the first swallows of civilization are starting to roost: Giesshübler mineral water, whisky, vermouth, Fernet-Branca. Together with the gold fillings and the New York slang, the half-education and the mandolins of the returnees from the States, together with the Fords in the streets suggestive of crushed barrel-organs, they constitute the transition from so-called "national culture" to the demand for an "autonomous republic".

Albania is *en route* from the vendetta to the League of Nations.

Frankfurter Zeitung, 15 June 1927

36

The Albanian Army
(1927)

The Albanian army exercises from five to twelve in the morning and from three to seven in the afternoon. It exercises during its lunch-break. It exercises before bedtime; and at night, when the soldiers are asleep, many hundreds of trumpets may be heard blowing in the mosques (in which the army likes to camp). From this I conclude that the Albanian army surely exercises in its sleep. I am forced to wonder, is there any time when the Albanian army is *not* exercising?

Nor do I know *why* it exercises. There seems to be an irresistible compulsion to exercise in the human male—I am the only exception I know of. The Albanian people are born fighters, and they like to shoot from infancy—why in the world would they still exercise? If the rest of us exercise, that's on account of some legal obligation or other. Our names appear on a roll, we are enlisted, we have to exercise or we are shot. We exercise, therefore, for dear life. In Albania there are no such legal obligations. Recruits are—so they are told—summoned for six months at a time, and are then free to go home. They are supposed to be paid, too. But the fact is that in Albania recruits are kept for two years, and they are not paid a penny—even the officers only manage to get three months of back-pay by extorting it (staff officers are permanently owed two months), and senior policemen live from the sale of confiscated goods—so why do they exercise in Albania? Moreover, deserters are not punished. Recruits, who, without a word to a soul go back to their villages, are handed over by the police to a passing motorist who happens to be stationed in the deserter's own garrison. The prospect of a ride in a Ford is enough to persuade the deserter to return to his unit, which is to say to return to his exercises. Discipline leaves nothing to be desired. Those soldiers who happen not to have deserted, stiffly and with evident enjoyment salute every passing officer—because who could force them to stiffness? They march, perform knee bends, turns, stand to attention, run, drop to their knees, run in "loose order" and don't get paid a penny, and their officers don't either. Why don't they desert? Why do they exercise?

Further, *to what end* do Albanian soldiers exercise? They know the mountains like the backs of their hands, they know all the hiding places, they can climb like mountain goats. Surely no one proposes to use them in a world war? A knee bend is unavailing against poison gas. Is Albania contemplating an invasion of Italy by any chance? Even if it were, it can't be done by exercises. Surely they would need to shoot? Now the Albanian army has Austrian rifles and Italian ammunition, bullets that jam, magazines that can't be clicked in, British knapsacks that can't be secured with Italian straps, covers for field-shovels and no field-shovels with which to dig trenches, Italian officers who don't know commands in Albanian, Austrian officers who are blackballed by their Italian comrades, White Russian officers who don't exercise at all, but have only come so as to be able to stay in uniform while they wait for Soviet Russia to collapse, British officers who know neither Albanian nor Italian nor German nor Russian, and like to walk around with their swizzle sticks just so that Britain is represented too. It's the oddest army in the world. It has no coherent rule book or command structure, all it has is martial music, trumpet signals, drums, and a devotion to drill. Men used to scampering in soft slippers over rocks have been shod in heavy, hobnailed boots that make it impossible for them to pick their feet up. They don't need heavy packs, because they can live on bread and cheese and water for months on end. But they are given heavy knapsacks with pointless contents on useless straps. They were forced to leave their own, Austrian ammunition at home, and were issued with Italian ammunition, because the contracts have gone to Milanese suppliers, so now they can't even shoot—as they could quite happily in civvy street. But they exercise.

For whom do they exercise? Surely not for their country? Because half the country is unhappy with their government—for reasons of idealism. Half the rest has been bought by the Serbs, and the remainder is on the payroll of the Italians. And in the middle of it, the soldiers are exercising. Perhaps they are exercising for Ahmed Zogu, their president? He has his personal bodyguard, which, if required to, will shoot at the regular soldiers, who, for all their exercising, are thought not to be reliable, and who are deliberately issued with bad ammunition and heavy boots, to keep them from undertaking anything against the president. Only the bodyguard has matching ammunition, no rucksacks, lightweight boots, a unified command structure and personal friends of the president to lead them.

So I repeat my questions: why, for whom, and to what end does the Albanian army exercise? All I am able to say is why:

Because they are stupid. Because they enjoy sweating, being yelled at, tormented and oppressed. I suspect that this is not confined to Albanians. The Europeans are no different. Did I say the Albanians had the oddest army in the world? It's not true. *All* armies in the world are odd; very odd.

Frankfurter Zeitung, 29 June 1927

37

Western Visitors in Barbaria
(1927)

One can infer the exotic character of Albania straightaway from the peculiar carry-on of the civilized Europeans there. The members of this curious race, whose baffling customs and practices have still not sufficiently been researched, and who make a point of hating each other in their comfortable homelands, seem in wild terrain to have taken on a different heart, a different point of view and a different character. Immediately after setting foot in a country without flushing toilets they unpack from their travelling bags a never-used, gleaming friendliness, to exchange it like for like with their equally civilized fellows. In particularly inhospitable areas, it seems real ladies have been seen dancing with commercial representatives in the European club—merely to break through the ranks of natives.

In Albania I am able to establish that all Europeans and Americans are one heart and one soul. Racial memories of liftboys and bundles of stocks and shares form an indissoluble bond that is finally cemented when a gramophone sounds and couples contort themselves to dance. Rival diplomats fight shoulder to shoulder against mosquitoes, malaria and the least attempt on the part of a native to approach the culture they are bringing him. All the rivals who have clustered round this tough but—until now—unspoken-for morsel, march together and take their profits separately. Even journalists generously pass on to one another their snippets of false news from real sources. Early in the morning you can see military attachés greeting a barber who happens to be in their sector, and hence at the mercy of their protection. Veritable excellencies leave calling cards at unimportant addresses. Outside the embassies are no dismissive guards but a humble policeman or *kavass*. Where in Europe an unmannerly secretary remains seated, here a friendly dragoman rises to his feet. Gentlemen are on occasion capable of sharing a bed together just to confuse the local bugs. The brother-liness of the masters is as great as it would be in the last hour before the end of the world. They tremble before the volcano on which they dance their Charlestons. A couple of distinguished locals have been adopted in the circle of the foreign gods. Tirana has a tennis club where anyone who swings a racket and uses toothpaste is admitted. An Albanian colonel and national hero of Austrian ancestry and Western character offers a welcome subject of conversation. A couple of Albanian officials venture on a round of cards with the wives of English officers. A German company director plays poker with the Vice Consul of a Balkan state. Americans are friendly to Bulgarians, because they have a deal to sell sponges to Sofia, and Tirana is not yet in the bag. The odd minister may be seen helping an *au pair* as she takes her little European charges on a walk.

On some evenings there are parties. The English, who would be instantly recognizable even in their lounge suits, come in tails. On one such evening it transpired that a feudal yachtsman who hates the press and indeed any piece of paper not bearing a coat of arms, sat down and talked to me for fully half an hour—which I did not recip-rocate. We drank whisky and soda, mixed by the White Russian who is running the bar here till such time as the czar is resurrected. People told each other stories. Because Tirana has gossip—the foreign gods don't even notice how humane they are being.

We hear that the attractive girlfriend of the Albanian president is a Viennese girl from Ottakring by the name of Franzi. She was seen driving a Fiat. When? This afternoon! What time? Twenty past four! What was she wearing? A new hat! Describe the hat! It was red! — Major X, adjutant of the President's sister, refused permission to a young Albanian official to dance with her. When the young man did anyway, the Major had him arrested. He spent three days in Tirana gaol. The barbarousness of it! splutter the foreign gods. Even though in Bavaria writers often spent years behind bars, without ever seeing an adjutant. In America Charlie Chaplin is boycotted because he kissed his wife on the mouth and elsewhere. In France, remember, there was a certain Dreyfus. In Italy individuals with sound digestion are made to guzzle castor oil. But Albania—Albania is unspeakable.

Diplomats have to prove they are representing their national interests. They hover—extraterritorial as they are—like flies on a cheese cloche, buzzing back and forth in large automobiles, pay calls on one another, snoop on one another, take counsel together, make mountains out of molehills, encode them, and wire them home. Then the situation becomes tense. There is a rush to arms. Then a journalist trots along to the telegraph office. He hears a toot. It was the horn of an ambassador. In the newspaper it was the fire brigade of our special correspondent. The newspaper eavesdrops on the diplomat. The diplomat believes what he reads. What have you heard? Armed bands in Scutari? Have you spoken to the military attaché? Haven't you heard? Salonica? Sazan? Gunboats? Hydroplanes?

In the meantime the Albanian peasants work their fields, the traders sell traditional *opanci* shoes, the blacksmiths hammer out saucepans, the saddlers stitch saddles. But every morning brings march-past, drums, reveille, knee-bends. Sooner or later, you're going to get shot. By the Italians? By the South Slavs? — Who cares? War is war.

Frankfurter Zeitung, 7 July 1927

38

Article about Albania
(Written on a Hot Day)
(1927)

Albania is beautiful, unhappy, and for all its current topicality, boring. Its mountains are sometimes of an uncertain clear substance, so that you might take them for shards of glass painted green. It's only on dull days, when the sky isn't clouded over so much as swaddled in a thin overcoat of cloudy stuff, that you feel they might be rock after all. They have become more massive, implacable, and the whole country feels like a locked courtyard, ringed by the walls of a natural prison. Freedom is a relative concept, you sense that there are no railways at hand to lead us into our century, that ships two hours, four hours, twelve hours from here, only put in once a week at an Albanian port, and the exoticism of it is twice as hard to bear as a self-chosen torment. Viewed from the distance of Berlin, the phenomenon of the vendetta may well appear worth investigating. On its native terrain, though, it rather blurs into the background of filth, cockroaches, dark nights, broken oil lamps, fat spiders, malaria attacks and murky seaweed tea.

Under such circumstances, I am less receptive to the beauties of nature than those born optimists called tourists. At most, I might register: quiet blue days of simple sublimity; a hot sun that bakes

even your shadow, and that is palpable in every cool recess; a few
birds (a rarity here, because the shooters are so assiduous) in the air
and of course also on the branches; forests of an unfathomable stillness, depth and darkness. A few houses, windowless, fortress-like,
deaf and blind cubes of stone, coarse, enigmatic and tragic, redolent of destiny and secret curses. On each of these buildings that are
so arranged as to offer rest to a murderer, refuge to a pursued man,
security to a whole clan, lies the so-called charm of eeriness, which
I would sooner not get too close to. Without the permission of the
master of the house, one may not set foot in the meanest hut. But
with his permission, the hospitality is life-threatening. Hospitality
is a fine custom, among the noblest proofs of humanity. But there
is every justification for it too in the selfish thought that among
people who have instituted blood revenge for justice, a man needs
to rest up somewhere, because sooner or later everyone will end up
as a fugitive. If you are resolute in your sceptical thinking, then you
will come to the conclusion that a good police force is actually
preferable to hospitality. May Albanians and others forgive me that
I am not sufficiently gifted to admire unproductive conservatism in
the way it should be admired. Unfortunately, alongside other habits
that I revere, the Albanians have one that I merely understand: they
are utterly intent on preserving old habits, not only stressing their
Albanianism at the expense of their humanity, but also cultivating
their tribalism at the expense of their nation. Albanians who live
outside Albania like to shut themselves away, marry only one
another, and remain suspicious of their new settings. Even in
America, they remain Albanians, talk to each other in Albanian, and
at the end of a few decades away, return, why?—in order to go
around in a cartridge belt in Albania. Like other small peoples, they
have that kind of national feeling that causes the nation to die and
keeps the national culture impoverished. Hence the fact that the
Albanian language still has no word for "love", no fixed terms for
the colours of the rainbow, no particular word for "God"; that

Albanian literature could be a richer or at the very least a more accurate representation of Albanian life today, but remains as simple as the first songs of European humanity and lags behind the development of even this laggardly country. The materials of the literature are bucolic family sagas. Alongside the patriotic conservatism, tribal rivalries exist at the expense of the nation, and religious fanaticism at the expense of religion. It's not as though the Albanians are particularly devout. But their membership of a faith in and of itself leads them to look askance at members of others.

I understand that most "national traits" are the consequence of an unhappy history, in this case centuries of bitter struggle against the Turks. But there were also thousands of Albanians who went voluntarily to serve the Turks, were Turkish favourites, generals, officials, helped oppress their country and—and yet remained Albanians. Such are the whims of national culture. An Albanian major said to me: "It's as well that the Turks oppressed us, and kept us away from their civilization. But for that, the Albanian language might have disappeared without trace." This was, as I say, an Albanian major speaking. Therefore I didn't say what I was sorely tempted to say: But what good did that do you? Try telling your beautiful wife: I love you in Albanian. Wouldn't it be better to say it wholly in Turkish than half-say it in Albanian? It's a crime to oppress a nation, we both agree about that. But to praise the negative outcome of this oppression, the chance survival of a technically interesting language is false and childish national pride. But as I say, I bit my tongue.

I passed through towns of an exquisite ghostliness, and others that were simply heart-breaking. I saw Elbasan, one of the oldest towns in the country. Its stone buildings in stone courtyards in stone grounds have the monumentality of death and at the same time its idyllic grief. There is nothing so moving as the green between stones, cracks and crannies sprouting soft, damp moss, the flower of mould and nothingness. It makes the stone somehow still stonier. With its winding lanes and its hunchbacked bazaar the town is reminiscent of a sort of huge and whimsically, defiantly irregular snail shell, whose original inhabitant has died and has left its place to a clutch of casual, brown, picturesquely clad, also soiled and broken traders. It appears that most of Elbasan belongs to one Shefgiet Verlaci, the father-in-law to be of Ahmet Zogu. Elbasan boasts one of the loveliest, widest, greenest prayer sites of the whole country, where on hot afternoons priests and acolytes like to recline and give themselves over to metaphysics. In the east are the great Mohammedan cemeteries with gravestones like outsize mushrooms; in the south is the dynamited bridge at Skumli, and further an extensive deep-green olive wood, a fairy-tale wood for a stage production.

I will mention Kruja. It is a dream of primitivism. It reminds me of the story of Rebecca going to the well. A naïve early Biblical fuzz overlies the overgrown village. Pots are baked in large fiery open ovens, Old Testament forms, handled jars of innocent clay, brown-ish-girlish, with youthfully slim necks and hips, and slightly clumsy thin spouts. Turkish coffee is boiled on open fires. The café consists of a *patron* and an immovable set of scales, in whose pans sit a couple of cups filled with black, viscous, syrupy stuff. The town is ruled with a heavy hand by the gendarmerie commander, who in another life was a warlord (or, some might say, robber baron). He has a fine uniform with gold stars.

Walking around, you encounter Biblical scenes: shepherds scarved against sunburn, leaf huts, tents of woven willow, men on mule-back, veiled women, knitting as they walk. The land is so peaceful that you refuse to credit its reputation for murder. Even so, I met a man who wanted to avenge a friend, and shot an innocent party by mistake. He was unlucky: the innocent party had seven brothers, who are now all on the tail of my acquaintance. He tried sending out various emissaries, but it takes a while to settle on a price. For three months now he has lived in imminent expectation of death. He is no sort of primitive Albanian either, but a man who has lived in Paris as a munitions worker and returned, expressly to carry out his vendetta. Even though he is himself pursued, he is still looking for the man who murdered his friend.

If you come to the European towns like Scutari, Valona, Korça, towns with stiff collars, cravats, postcards, razor blades, gold fillings, Ford automobiles and lawyers—then you are even less inclined to believe in such a proximity of semi-civilization and epic. Even so, the barber's brother is a bone fide and quite a successful warlord. When he comes into town, he has himself shaved, drinks coffee, and talks like you and me. We're all human.

Urban Albanians are strikingly timid. It takes less courage to shoot here than to speak. An Albanian would rather shoot than say what he thinks. He is afraid of the walls' ears. He senses a spy in everyone, and he's half-right. An Albanian "Okhrana" in the sense of the Russian organization doesn't exist—not least because every urban Albanian is a passionate and spontaneous observer of his neighbours' comings and goings and doings, takes childlike pleasure in teasing out "mysteries" and finds dangerous secrets in perfectly open and transparent things. This complicates life for the good Albanian people. A stranger does not come in for particular attention, no, everyone watches him with passion and primitive fascination. How often I met Albanians who said to me, with cunning expressions on their faces: "You're a journalist"—as though I had tried to make a secret of it, and should now feel rumbled. But if I happened to ask: "What's new then?" or "What does it say in your Albanian newspaper that I can't read?" then they shrugged their shoulders, because "new" is equated with danger, and anything resembling a "novelty" may give you away. A constant formula is the reply: "I have no news. You tell me something. You know everything." Then you can be sure that your discreet Albanian will straightaway repair to some interesting place and report: "What he said was …" These people's love of intrigue is as great as their fear of expressing an opinion. Over time, they do so little that they seem to have given up all their own opinions, and only listen to those of others. Why have an opinion merely to suppress it? In place of political convictions there is political partisanship, instead of struggle conspiracy, instead of a word a hint, instead of caution fear. In this land no ruler is safe, and no subject either. A publicly expressed view is an impossibility—even if it were allowed. Over the centuries the Albanians have lost all pleasure in the right to an opinion. Even unambiguous circumstances become secret mysteries in their hands. They have no taste for the absence of danger.*

Their virtues are courtesy, silence, modesty, gentleness. Their most dangerous quality: love of money. There are places where the farmers bury piles of gold, and continue to acquire more. Perhaps their frugality is half miserliness. They are not so much work-shy as plain feeble. They accomplish vastly less than a European because they are so poorly nourished. Their lack of wants borders on the absurd. Their extreme moderation is sad and oppressive— almost as oppressive as the absence of women in the public life of the towns, where you can go many days without seeing or hearing a single one. Their lives are de-eroticized, love has been degraded to a domestic virtue, and a stroll is as perspectiveless as a Sunday.

But such a topical part of the world ... !

Frankfurter Zeitung, 30 July 1927

---

* For an insider's up-to-date account of this superbly paranoid state of affairs and state, see Ismail Kadare's *The Successor*.

Part VI

Hotels

39

Arrival in the Hotel
(1929)

The hotel that I love like a fatherland is situated in one of the great port cities of Europe,* and the heavy gold Antiqua letters in which its banal name is spelled out (shining across the roofs of the gently banked houses) are in my eye metal flags, metal bannerets that instead of fluttering blink out their greeting. Other men may return to hearth and home, and wife and child; I celebrate my return to lobby and chandelier, porter and chambermaid—and between us we put on such a consummate performance that the notion of merely checking into a hotel doesn't even raise its head. The look with which the doorman welcomes me is more than a father's embrace. As though he actually were my father, he discreetly pays my taxi out of his own waistcoat pocket, saving me from having to think about it. The receptionist emerges from his glass booth with a smile as wide as his bow is deep. My arrival seems to delight him so much that his back imparts friendliness to his mouth, and the professional and the human are mingled in his greeting. He would be ashamed to greet me with a registration form; so deeply does he understand the way I see the legal require-

---

* The hotel's identity—if it has one, and is not a composite or a dream—is not known. Helmuth Nürnberger conjectures that the gently shelving port city may be Marseilles.

ment as a personal insult. He will fill in my details himself, later on, when I am installed in my room, even though he has no idea where I have come from. He will write out some name or other, some place he thinks deserving of having been visited by me. He is a greater authority on my personal data than I am. Probably over the years namesakes of mine have stayed in the hotel. But he doesn't know their details, and they seem a little suspicious to him, as if they were unlawful borrowers of my name. The liftboy takes my suitcases one under each arm. Probably it's the way an angel spreads his wings. No one asks me how long I plan on staying, an hour or a year, my fatherland is happy either way. The reception-ist whispers into my ear: "627! Is that all right?"—as if I could picture the room to myself as he can.

Well, and in fact I can! I love the "impersonal" quality of that room, as a monk may love his cell. And as other men may be happy to be reunited with their pictures, their china, their silver, their chil-dren and their books, so I rejoice in the cheap wallpaper, the spotless ewer and basin, the gleaming hot and cold taps, and that wisest of books: the telephone directory. My room of course never faces the back. It is the room of a "regular", so it has no facing room and yet looks out over the street. Opposite are a chimney, the sky, and a cloud ... But it's not so secluded that the condensed melody of the large nearby square doesn't reach up to me like an echo of the dear world; so that I am by myself but not isolated, alone but not forgotten, private but not abandoned. I have only to open the window, and the world steps in. From afar I hear the hoarse sirens of ships. Very near are the jaunty ting-a-lings of trams. Car horns seem to call me by name—they greet me, as they might a senator. The policeman at the heart of it orders the traffic. The newspaper boys toss the names of their newspapers into the air like so many balls. And little street scenes enact themselves for me like a series of playlets. A slight pressure on the Bakelite bell-push and a green light goes on in a back corridor, signal for the room-service waiter.

And here he is already! His professional eagerness is confined to his tail-coat—in his breast under the starched shirt front is human warmth; preserved for me, kept safe for the whole duration of my absence. When he telephones my order through to the kitchen so many floors below, he doesn't forget to add who it is for, so that the sound of my name in the cook's memory may spark some recollection of my particular preferences. The waiter smiles. He has no need of speech. He has no need to check or confirm anything. There is no possibility of any error. I am already so familiar to him that he would be prepared to accept tips from me on credit—at a suitable rate of interest, of course. His faith in the inexhaustible sources of my income is itself inexhaustible. And if I should one day turn up in rags and as a beggar, he would take that for an ingenious form of disguise. He knows I am merely a writer. But still he gives me credit.

I pick up the telephone. Not to make a call—only to say hello to the hotel telephonist. He puts me through promptly and often. He says I am out, if required. He warns me. In the morning he relays important news items to me from the paper. And when there is money on the way, he lets me know with discreet jubilation. He is an Italian. The waiter is from Upper Austria. The porter is a Frenchman from Provence. The receptionist is from Normandy. The head waiter is Bavarian. The chambermaid is Swiss. The valet is Dutch. The manager is Levantine; and for years I've suspected the cook of being Czech. The guests come from all over the world. Continents and seas, islands, peninsulas and ships, Christians, Jews, Buddhists, Muslims and even atheists are all represented in this hotel. The cashier adds, subtracts, counts and cheats in many languages, and changes every currency. Freed from the constriction of patriotism, from the blinkers of national feeling, slightly on holiday from the rigidity of love of land, people seem to come together here and at least appear to be what they should always be: children of the world.

Before long I will go downstairs—to complete my arrival. The receptionist will come up to tell me his news and to hear mine. His interest is devoted to me as entirely as that of the astronomer in the first hour of a comet's appearance over the horizon. Have I changed? Can I be said to be the same? His eye, delicate and precise as a telescope, takes in the material of my suit, the cut of my boots—and the assurance: "I'm delighted to see you looking so well, sir!"—refers not so much to my state of health as to the apparent state of my finances. Yes, you're the same as ever—he might equally have said.—Thank God you haven't sunk so far that you might have to seek out another hotel. You are our guest and our child! And long may you remain so!

My interest meanwhile is in everything concerning the hotel, as though I stood one day to inherit shares in it. How's business? What ships are expected this month? Is the old waiter still alive? Has the manager been unwell? No international hotel thieves, I trust? — In that one fine hour those are my concerns. I should like to be shown the books, and check the reservations for the months ahead. Am I in any way different from a man whom love of country prompts to check the budget of his nation, the political orientation of the cabinet, the health of the head of state, the organization of the police force, the equipment of the armed forces, the number of the navy's cruisers? I am a hotel citizen, a hotel patriot.

Before long the moment comes when the receptionist reaches into a distant pigeonhole and pulls out a bundle of letters, telegrams and periodicals for me. A glance shoots out in my direction, in advance of my post. The letters are out of date and nevertheless new. They have been waiting for me for a long time. I know already some of their contents, having been apprised of them by other means. But who knows?! Among the expected letters may be one that surprises me, perhaps unhinges me, or causes my life to change its course? How can the receptionist stand there calmly smiling as he hands me my mail? His equanimity is the product of long experience, of a bittersweet paternal wisdom. He is sure that nothing surprising will come, he understands the monotony of a hectic life; no one knows as well as he does the absurdity of my vague romantic notions. He knows passengers by their luggage, and letters by their envelopes. "Your mail, sir!" he says coolly. And yet his hand, as it delivers the bundle into my keeping, bows, as it were, at the wrist, in accordance with an ancient tradition, a ritual of receptionists' hands ...

I pull up a chair in the lobby. It is home and the world, foreign and familiar, my ancestorless gallery! Here I will start to write about my friends, the hotel personnel. Such characters they are! Cosmopolites! Students of humanity! Expert readers of languages and souls! No Internationale like theirs! They are the true internationals! (Patriotism only begins with the owners of the hotel.)

I will begin by describing my friend, the receptionist.

Frankfurter Zeitung, 9 January 1929

40

The Chief Receptionist
(1929)

I n the afternoon "between trains", when the lobby is quiet and empty and an idyllic golden light floods the reception area, the chief receptionist reminds me of a kind of gold-braid and mobile saint in an iconostasis. To complete the likeness, he folds his hands over the little golden buttons that retain his belly, and commits himself to a profound contemplation of the air, the play of dust motes, and probably a few thoughts on his home life. Eventually he feels a pang at his inactivity in front of his boys, who are standing around in a small group, and in whom the unruliness of youth may at any moment stir, and so he contrives a few activities, in themselves highly superfluous but of a suggestively exemplary nature, to improve morale. He takes the heavy gold watch out of his waistcoat pocket and compares its time with that shown on the electric wall clock, whose great, round, white face hangs there like a hotel moon on two coarsely woven chains, accenting the golden afternoon with its ghostly silver. It is so quiet that each time the big hand marks a minute one hears the click, almost human in the silence. For a long time the receptionist looks at the two chronometers, as though to catch one out by a second or two. Then with a resolute expression that is the visual equivalent of a sigh, he returns his watch to its pocket. He lays two large books over each other in such a way that their edges are exactly aligned, slides the telephone half an inch closer to the inkwell, with the flat of his hand trundles the pen into its designated hollow, examines a loose button on his cuff, and twists at it, to satisfy himself that it is in no imminent danger of falling off. No one dares disturb him. In this almost meditative hour, his assistants, a couple of fellows in grey, standing silently at the entrance, dare not approach him with a question.

There are always two different fellows posted by him, and by my reckoning there are six in all. I can't quite be sure, because I've never seen them all at the same time. When one lot arrives, the others are just setting off to consulates, chemists, florists, apartments, all about other people's business as messengers, agents or servants. For years I have been unable to establish whether they are hotel employees or personal friends of the chief receptionist's. By all appearances, it is he and not it that is their bread-giver and the dictator of their opportunities. They obey him as hunting dogs obey the master of hounds—and no matter how far away they are on their errands, it's always as though he had them on invisible, elasticated strings, and could reach them at any moment. He treats them like a kind of decayed relation or hereditary disease. There is undeniably something perplexing about their existence—a life without uniform and without badge. Everyone else here wears the sign of their service and their function, only they have retained the anonymity of mufti, which puts one in mind of the borders of legality, and a sort of frenzy, a pursued pursuit, of police and of forbidden paths.

But enough of them! In this quiet hour they don't exist for the chief receptionist, they are less than the air, which he at least deigns to contemplate. He avoids looking at them, even when talking to them. He has the gift of calling down an errand from the elevation of his box without looking at any particular individual. It is as though the lobby is full of minions only waiting for an assignment. Only when a guest steps up to his desk to make an order does he gently incline his head—not the better to hear it, but only to disguise his superiority which guests do not like to have their attention drawn to.

Because, make no bones about it, he is their superior. I find in his
powerful head, the wide white brow, where the hair at the temples
is already beginning to silver, the wide-set pale-grey eyes above
which the heavy eyebrows form two complete arches, the deep-
lying root of the powerful, beaky nose, the large and down-curving
mouth, shaded as the eyes by their brows by the curve of the pendulous pepper-and-salt moustache, the massive chin at the heart of
which is a lost little dimple that has survived from childhood: for
me this face echoes the portraits of great noblemen, a fixed expression of proud aloofness, an aura that spreads over the whole visage
like a transparent layer of bitter frost. The face is a reddish brown,
as though it came from a life out of doors, a life among wheat,
water, wood and wind, the skin is taut—and the handful of deep
frown lines above the nose, and the more delicate pleats around the
eyes seem not to have come from the daily round of cares, but willingly accepted signs, tattoos administered by life and experience,
and performed by wind and weather ...

He bends down before the gentlemen but it is not a bow, but a
physical condescension. As he accepts an instruction it is as though
he were hearing a petition. When he nods in agreement, he
reminds one of the merciful judges in American films (which are
the only places where one sees merciful judges). The visitor is
unhappy about something now. But it looks as though the chief
receptionist is thinking about whose responsibility it is. And with
a small, utterly tangential question he is plucked from his consci-
entiousness into a kind of sympathy, and a remissness becomes
partiality. As though the gentleman were come to him not to complain about him but to voice a complaint to him. "Oi!" the chief
receptionist shouts down to the group of idle boys. "Which of you
took 375's suit to be ironed?" — Silence. It wasn't any of the boys,
but the porter whom the receptionist has just sent on a bus to the
station. He very well remembered the porter's protest the suit, the
particular urgency of the errand. But he doesn't for a moment feel

guilty. I'm not saying he has no conscience, but it is of a different quality. It is more spacious, like a general's maybe, preoccupied with more important things, full of concern for the whole enterprise. "On your way, and pick up the suit!" he orders. Who would give anything for the boy who ventured to ask: Where is it? Something is aroused now in the eye of the receptionist, something like the crack of the whip in a circus, a drawn poniard, a storm darkening on the horizon … The boy doesn't stop to ask, he runs off straightaway. A brooding silence settles on the remaining boys, a clouded summer sultriness. The master of the gold braid stands all alone in his elevation, and exhales a cloud of pure silent anger into the lobby.

Even so, he would straightaway break into a smile if a guest, for example myself, were to approach him now with a request. Nothing about him—and I certainly don't understand him to the degree that I perhaps appear to—nothing about him is as remarkable as his gift of switching almost instantaneously between fury and graciousness, indifference and curiosity, cool aloofness and anxiety to be of service. It's as though each of his feelings is lined with its obverse, and that all he needs to do is turn his mood around to transform himself. Now, ten minutes before the first guests are due off the Milan express, he moves into reception mode, which is to say, he gives a little tug at his waistcoat. "Ten minutes!" he calls out to the clerk. Then something remarkable happens: he leaves his receptionist's eyrie. He climbs down and scatters the group of boys, each of whom now runs to his allotted place, one to the revolving doors, another to the luggage elevator, a third to the lift for persons, another to the staircase, a couple more to the cloakroom. Two more minutes, and the first automobile draws up. The chief receptionist purses his lips and issues a snake-like hiss. From a dark side entrance a baggage man in green apron sprints up. Already the humming engine of a motor-car is audible outside. Here come the first pieces of luggage. The receptionist gives them a glance, and since they are leather and there is a dark grey and green tartan rug with them, and a leather-lined pouch for walking sticks and umbrellas, he gives another tug at his waistcoat. With each new arrival he exchanges a look with the reception clerk, and each glance signifies a room number, a floor, a price, an exhortation, a warning, affability or dourness. Yes, there are some guests at whose appearance the chief receptionist gently closes one eye, with the result they are told the hotel has no vacancies. Sometimes—but this happens once a week at most—the chief receptionist makes a bow, and when he is upright again, one sees his face wreathed in smiles, smiles that, like yawns, are contagious. Then the visitor proceeds past beaming faces, as between two rows of lit lamps.

By the bye, on this occasion I see that the chief receptionist has on a pair of grey worsted trousers, evidently the lower half of a well-cut suit, under his uniform tunic, as though to hint that only his upper half, the half with which he so rarely bows, is in livery. He tells me a little about his personal life, which I thought I knew something about. One more revelation, I imagine to myself. Certainly he has a relationship with a seamstress, and one may even assume that tailors are interested in his custom, and supply him with cut-price clothes. In the evening at six our friend disappears into the wardrobe, to emerge five minutes later in transformed dignity. For the first time one may see him responding to greetings. Taking his black silver-tipped cane in his grey-gloved left hand, with his right he touches the half top hat which he continues to affect, doffs it politely but quickly to his boys, who all bow very low to him. He has a little comradely chat with the night porter. Visitors who are sitting in the lobby or who happen to cross his path he doesn't even look at. Once more his eyes sweep the room, spot me, and send me a little spurt of friendliness. Then he enters the revolving door. And from the slow majesty with which it spins one may tell who has just left the hotel.

Frankfurter Zeitung, 24 January 1929

41

The Old Waiter
(1929)

This waiter is so old that he is known all over the hotel as "the old man", and employees and guests alike refer to him as "the old man", and he himself probably only intermittently recollects his name, which has fallen into disuse over many years. It's as though he had none any more, because like a mythological demi-god he has joined the ranks of those whose names no longer matter, because they represent a function. The waiter represents age in this hotel—and, as a distant second, waiterdom. He was a waiter for over forty years, now he has been "old" for another ten. And the set of tails he pulls on every afternoon has changed from professional to emblematic clothing—if you see the waiter in them, you think that that is the fitting uniform for old age.

I should say that this old man bears none of the familiar badges of old age. He is clean shaven, his skull is completely hairless, and even his eyebrows have remained pale, by some freak of nature. He seems to have refused the respectable silver of old age. Either that, or he is so old that he has passed through the epoch of white hair and is well on the way to petrifaction, a species of human mineral, perhaps regressing to the world's original condition, the inertness of the so-called inorganic. If you watch him leaning against one of the stout pillars in the hotel lobby for an hour, a stubby clay pipe (extinguished) in the corner of his mouth, lower lip pouting, his slightly pendulous cheeks the gleaming waxy red of some Tyrolean apples, his little expressionless eyes of shiny cobalt fixing some distant world, his crisp shirtfront of a pure, almost otherworldly white, the deep black of the impeccably fitting tails without a crease or speck of dust, in his gleaming shoes the steady reflections of lamps and candles— then you might suppose the waiter was his own monument, a deity of the hotel and the tourist trade, and you would feel unable to pass him without a small bow. But then all at once—and just when you least expect it, he starts to move—and the sight is so improbable that you start to wonder about the pillar as well, and suspect that it too will shortly change location. Where is the old man going? — To the restaurant. He walks from the knees down, his feet take tiny shuffling steps, if someone is in his way, he will stop, a mechanism stalls, and you think you hear somewhere under the tails that a little cog has suddenly ground to a halt. Then he starts to move again. A quarter of an hour later, the old man reaches the restaurant.

He never moves—though this is not always immediately apparent—without some end in view. Guests have arrived whom he waited on twenty or thirty years before and whose approach he saw while he was leaning against the pillar, his eyes apparently fixed on some other world. His alertness is unchanged, only his movements have slowed down. This was how he watched people arriving forty years before. Only then he got there quicker, he materialized in front of them, he ran to the kitchen, he was back. Imperceptibly but steadily over the years and the decades his feet have grown feebler, his hands more shaky, his movements slower; imperceptible as the movement of an hour hand on a clock, but just as unstoppable, age and feebleness have overtaken the body of the old waiter. Every day his walk has grown a little slower—till finally at the end of forty years it has become a glacial shuffle.

Now he is standing before his familiar guests, a bow is something he can still manage. A second waiter, a young and nimble one, is at the side of the old man, pad in hand, ready to take the order.

It's as though the old guests spoke in a language that the young waiter doesn't understand, the language of a vanished generation, perhaps a vanished world. For the old man repeats everything the guests have said verbatim to his young colleague—but it looks as though he were interpreting it. It is as though the orders were only turned into edible dishes, to courses, to delicacies, by grace of the old waiter's intervention. If the young fellow were to take them down directly, they might prove to be inedible. Although the guests speak softly (the table they are seated at an oasis of silence in the room full of noise and talk and clattering plates and clinking glasses), the old man hears every word of what they have to say— the young one presumably wouldn't be capable of it. For the former has the gift of intuition; he guesses what the guests want— and further, he is capable of changing their order should he choose to do so. For it is possible that they might order a dish whose quality on a given day the old man is unwilling to vouch for. Then he will pretend they have ordered something else. And that is why the guests are willing to wait for him while he slowly approaches their table. There is an ancient relationship between them and him, they are all coevals; just as one might share a certain provenance, they and he are, so to speak, patriots of an epoch, which is a dearer and more important thing than a fatherland anyway, because times are quick to disappear, while fatherlands remain what they were; one can cast aside or mislay the former, while the latter keep us in their grasp. The guests and the old waiter: they share the language of a gone epoch. That's why they understand one another, that's why they wait on and for one another.

It happens sometimes that an ancient old lady with the icy, dismissive look that is the consequence of a long, rich and carefree life, with a cane on which she leans, garbed in a matronly dress of dark grey silk, a lustrous pearl necklace (on which the heirs are already waiting) round her wrinkled neck—that this timidly or respectfully treated lady makes straight for the old waiter, and without a word, gives him her hand. Then he will bow deeply and smile distantly. The old and by all indications frosty lady and the waiter have known each other for decades—and she will not always have given him her hand in that time. When they were both still young, the separations of caste stood between them. Now that they have grown old a process of levelling has begun that will end in the equality of death. Already both are preparing for the grave, the same earth, the same dust, the same worms—maybe even, if faith has managed to survive such a long life—the same hereafter.

At one in the morning, the old man gets into the lift—not the service lift, the one for guests—and has himself taken up to the top floor. There he occupies a small room, a grace and favour room. He has never been married, has no children, no brothers or sisters. He was always alone, a waiter in the hotel, a child of the hotel. Never more than a waiter. He has occupied his room for ten years now. He didn't want to retire. He was no longer capable of braving the street and going home at the end of the day. So, like an old grandfather clock, he stayed in the hotel. One day he will die in his grace and favour room. No question. His body will be carried out through the hotel's service entrance and loaded into a black car without windows. Because it's not conceivable that one could transport a body through the lobby of the hotel.

Frankfurter Zeitung, 27 January 1929

42

The Cook in his Kitchen
(1929)

Of uncommon significance, though invisible, yes, unknown to most, the cook dwells in the underworld of the hotel. Most of the day he spends sitting in the middle of his big kitchen, in a glass-walled pavilion, a little hut, in other words, made entirely of glass, visible from all sides, seeing to all sides. The underworld of the hotel is composed of these three elements: glass, tiles, and a white, silvery, matte metal. A fourth is water, pouring incessantly, quietly, melodiously, over the white tiled walls, continually alert and soothing at the same time, a delicate, glittering veil of bridal-hygienic innocence, precious, prodigal, and in places where the light falls, rainbow-coloured.

Eight cooks and four trainee cooks stand and run about, arrayed in white, with snow-white sailors' caps on their heads, wooden spoons in their hands, at eight metal cauldrons, from which at irregular intervals silvery steam rises and in whose underbellies a reddish, unreal, theatrical fire glows. A never-ending white silence, comparable to the silence of the Russian taiga, blows over the tiles, the metal, the glass and the cooks, whose movements are inaudible, like those of white shadows, and whose footfall is probably swallowed up by the sound of the rushing water. This, the only sound in the room, doesn't break the silence, merely accompanies it; it seems to be the audible melody of silence, the song of muteness.

Ever so occasionally the vent of a cauldron allows a suppressed hiss to escape which straightaway dies down, shocked and ashamed and soon forgotten in the stillness, like the choked caw, say, of a raven in the white depthless silence of winter.

The kitchen might be the engine room of a modern ghost-ship. The cook might be a captain. The cooks the seamen. The trainees cabin boys. The destination unknown and in point of fact unreachable.

As dreamy as the silence is, that's how real, bright and alive the cook is in his festive, material, palpable optimism. Just watching him is enough to make one forget all the bad stories one's heard and exchange them for cheery memories of fairy tales, of Cockaigne for instance, of enchanting, brightly coloured illustrations in books. Here is the creator of the roast chickens that go flying into your mouth. His white brimless top hat of striped canvas, equally reminiscent of a turban, night-cap, and the underlining of a royal crown, deepens the natural russet of his cheeks, the lustrous metallic black of his dense, bushy eyebrows, and the golden brown of his small, darting eyes, that playfully move over his comfortable cheeks, supervise the sous-chefs, watch the cauldrons, pursue the movements of the long spoons. In its crooked exuberance the hat grazes his red, throbbing, right ear, which seems to manifest an optimism all of its own. His red lips are set in an unvarying smile. The broad soft chin is bedded on a comfortable jowl. The broad nostrils sniff the smells of the dishes and the nuances of the smells. And under the white apron curves his capacious and benevolent belly, where a second and particular heart would find room.

That's what I call a cook! He seems to step straight out of my childhood dreams, though in reality, as I believe I have already intimated, he is from Czechoslovakia. Of the four nationalities that live in that country, the Czechs, the Germans, the Slovaks and the Jews, he unites all the positive qualities: he has the application of the Czech, the method of the German, the imagination of the Slovak, and the cunning of the Jew. This ideal mixture makes for a contented, kindly man who lives at ease with others and himself, who is even capable of having a harmonious marriage over decades. Absurd, the very idea that he might fly into a temper! Where would rage find a place in somewhere already so filled with peace, contentment and freedom from care! And what would need to happen to knock this man off kilter? On the little table where he mostly sits, there is a large open diary in which he occasionally scribbles a note, and next to it a telephone that rings as often as twenty times an hour. Each time the cook picks up the receiver with the same tranquillity, he picks it up while it is still ringing, lays it carefully on the table, lets it rasp a little longer, and only when it has gone quite still does he lift it with a casual movement of the forearm not to his ear but to the proximate vicinity of his ear. It looks as though he first tames an unruly, noisy creature before agreeing to involve himself with it. He doesn't, like all the world, speak into the tube, but again only into its vicinity, and he doesn't raise his voice by half a degree, if anything he lowers it a little, and then the words he speaks to the telephone are all of velvet. Every quarter of an hour or so one of the four kitchen boys comes into the glass pavilion bearing a minuscule sample of food from one of the cauldrons on a small dish. Sometimes it is enough for the cook to cast one of his hurried golden glances at it (as if his eye can taste) and approve the dish with a gentle nod. Often, though, the cook raises the dish to his mouth, licks at it with his tongue, and sends the boy back with a quiet word or two. Why he only looks here and tastes there is his own secret. I imagine he knows the whims of the cauldrons very well and the abilities of the cooks, and also he would do damage to his tongue if he over-exercised it. It is a very precious tongue, it has the versedness of a colossally pampered palate, and also the ability to feed a stomach. Because very often the cook will eat nothing all evening, without feeling hungry. He never eats in the kitchen. He only takes off his white uniform, his roomy white uniform, and then stands there in a dark suit. He takes his hat off, and he has thick, curly hair, and a white smooth forehead. Over his poplin shirtfront, masking his collar, is the small grey silk bow tie with black dots. Its delicate coquettish wings tone down the gravity of his appearance, and give the cook a look of something enterprising, dashing and boyish. He walks into the dining room. A corner table is reserved for him next to the pillar. He is served silently and with élan, he doesn't even need to order. He is given tiny portions that lie on the plate like so many precious stones. Slabs of meat would offend the cook. He eats gracefully and effortlessly and doesn't even need to dab his lips with a napkin. After his coffee he takes a small cognac. Before pouring, the waiter shows him the bottle. Sometimes the cook will silently take the bottle from the waiter's hands and set it down on his table. However tiny the little glasses are, he will only drink a few drops at a time. Then he gets up with effortless grace, not like a man who has been eating and drinking heavily, but as though he had been resting in a forest clearing in the morning, and is now walking out towards the sun. From a thin oval cigarette he blows blue fragrant clouds.

He goes home. He has a nice house, three children, an attractive young wife whose picture he keeps in the drawer of the table in the glass pavilion next to the put-away diary. He let me see her once. I'm sure he doesn't show the picture to anyone else, and only sees it each time he opens or closes the drawer and he gives her a quick caress. He has never loved another woman and he isn't the man to succumb to a sudden infatuation. (His salary is higher than the hotel manager's.) Before the war he worked in many of the world's great cities. Always in an atmosphere of tiles, glass, water and silvery metal. He went to war in 1914, calmly, without zeal and without fear, because he knew his uncommon gift would not fail to make an impression on the general staff officers. For four years he sat a dozen miles behind the front, in idyllic villages, with hot saucepans and abundant supplies. Sometimes he talks about that time. He never forgets to add: "The gentlemen on my staff dined better than they fought." It's the only aphorism that's ever occurred to him. It will last him to the end of his days, and it's meant as praise not blame. Once I asked him if he had been back to visit his newly independent homeland. "No," he said, "there's no need. This is where I pay my taxes." I asked him whether he wanted his son to follow him into the profession. "Maybe!" replied the cook. "If he has the talent." But there was doubt in his gentle voice. Perhaps, like many, he thinks the sons of geniuses turn out badly.

Frankfurter Zeitung, 3 February 1929

43

"Madame Annette"
(1929)

When Annette turned twenty-eight and still hadn't found a husband, she went to one of the jewellers in the Rue de la Providence in whose windows wedding bands of gold and silver and *doublé* by the dozen are looped over little velvet turrets, suggestive of tiny shimmering monuments to monogamy. She bought herself a silver wedding ring and put it on her left ring finger, in accordance with the practices of her country. She may have thought in the privacy of her own soul that one day a husband would present himself, and she would be able to exchange the silver ring for a golden one. For the time being, though, the silver one was sufficient, so to speak, as a way of putting God on notice, as moral compulsion exerted on Fate, so that it might at long last see fit to give her a spouse. Beyond that, the ring had one other, immediate function: it was able to keep the girl from the attentions of undesirable men, who are usually cowards *en plus*, by implying the presence of a jealous and strongly built husband lurking somewhere. It also won her a measure of respect with her female colleagues. Indeed, shortly after Annette had purchased the ring, the staff, which previously had called her "Mademoiselle Annette", took to calling her "Madame Annette". This might be the place to observe that the title of dame still impresses the odd spinster from a good family nowadays, who doesn't have the sorry prospect of serving strangers for a living; how much more, then, a girl who is supposed to remain so all her life, even if she should have become a grandmother! — To Annette's colleagues, who had so little occasion to call each other "Madame", that title conferred a social distinction. They bestowed it on Annette, even though they half-guessed that the silver ring was merely for appearances. They felt themselves ennobled when they were able to say "Madame Annette".

She had been in service since her fifteenth birthday. Her father, a Normandy fisherman, sent her to a small hotel in Le Havre, to whose landlady he had had old ties from when he had been a sailor. It would appear that girls are not readily countenanced in Le Havre. Less than a month after her arrival, Annette succumbed to the belated love-lowings of a fifty-year-old shipper, who promised to marry her, and was only kept from doing so by a marriage of twenty years. Annette got a baby, and shortly afterwards a good job with some blue-blooded people outside Paris, who were originally from Normandy themselves, and who liked to recruit their staff from there. The baby was left with the landlady in Le Havre, as a paying guest, and therefore died some six months later. Annette sent money for the funeral, and, not having a picture of her child, but wanting to remember him in some way, bought a postcard of a bonny infant in a *papeterie*, put it in a black frame, and kept it hidden away in her trunk.

Taught a lesson by her experience in Le Havre, and persuaded in her Norman-rustic way that any affair was bound to result in pregnancy, Annette fought off the wooings of M. de L., her new master—even though she did so with some reluctance. To save herself once and for all from temptation, she proceeded to tell Mme de L. of the attempts of her husband. As a result, how could it be otherwise, Annette was terminated straightaway, and, lest she create further confusion in another noble house, she was recommended to a large hotel in Paris, where a certain M. de L. sat on the board.

Here began her modest career.

She (not altogether mistakenly) thought it pleasanter in the course of a morning to clean twenty rooms of unknown and constantly changing persons, than eight or ten thoroughly established for all eternity, on whom she depended for bread and keep. She preferred tips, left behind like a form of tax by those departing, to a Christmas gift handed over with all ceremony by the lady of the house in December, and still made much of in April, at Easter. She became used to her job, because it lacked the monotony of a servant's; had none of the shabby lustre of a patriarchal disposition, but something of the cold, clear objectivity of a trade, almost of an office; and because in addition it gave her a sense of the diversity and colour of the world, its riches and its inhabitants. Because she was observant and quick on the uptake, she attained over time an understanding of the various habits of various circles, various degrees of intimacy with luxury, with life in a culture and a nobility that has its economic foundation. These experiences raised her expectations of those men she happened to meet. And even though she liked one or other of them, she could not decide to marry any of them. The only man she met at a dance who seemed to master the arts of a gentleman, which in the opinion of the chambermaids are the preserve of the upper classes, was a zouave, a corporal from the French colonies. She was frankly a little afraid of coloured gentlemen. If a man was yellow or black, surely it was bound to show one day, be it in the form of an outbreak of madness, a sudden act of violence or just an exotic malady. Still, she was all set to take the plunge. Then war broke out, and her zouave gave his life, as was proper, for Alsace-Lorraine.

Her grief was greater than her love had ever been, because she endowed the dead man with greater gifts than the living one had had. She remained convinced that she had lost the embodiment of manliness. Compared to her image of the dead man, the hotel guests were so many botched jobs. Even boxers and aviators were left trailing by her zouave. Not having his photograph, and as idealized pictures of zouaves were not offered on sale, she endowed him with all the traits of all the heroes whose pictures she saw in illustrated newspapers. In her pious brain that over the course of a few years did all the work that normally was performed by generations in the making of a legend, the departed became a coloured demi-god. Her memory of him kept her safe, it should be noted, from the seduction attempts of white, half-drunk and irresponsible hotel-guests.

If one has a great sorrow, it is a good thing to change one's abode. She came here, to the hotel I am writing about, basically because it is owned by the same company as the hotel in Paris. This is where she bought her wedding band, this is where she became known as Madame Annette, and as a consequence, came into an easier roster of duties. She is now, so to speak, the right hand of the housekeeper, has only five or six rooms to clean, and the girls on two floors under her wing. She no longer wears a blue dress, but a black one, and is not compelled to wear the customary white bonnet. But she likes to wear it just the same—out of a coquettishness she claims is modesty. She is extremely pretty. Yes, it seems to me that sometimes she doesn't realize herself how beautiful she is capable of being. Because to be aware of one's own beauty requires free time and a measure of material independence. Sometimes I think a man must tell her:

"Listen to me, Madame Annette (or even just plain Annette!), with your black hair, your pale grey eyes and your tan complexion you are a rare composition of nature. Even though you only wear silk stockings on Wednesdays, which are your day off, one can observe the charming curve of your leg on other days as well, the soft transition from the muscle of the calf to the sinew of the ankle. Don't imagine that your narrow hips, small breasts and strong, hard-working but shapely hands mark you out to the observer as not belonging to the social class you take for superior. You are easily capable of passing for a lady, even when you are just taking instructions, your bright eyes on a guest and then lingering in the empty space behind his turned back, your narrow, strangely red mouth (for which, with your complexion, you should really use a lighter shade of lipstick) pressed shut, as though to ward off any inappropriate behaviour, and your soft chin slightly upraised, as though that was the seat of attention, but also of pride. There's no doubting your beauty, Annette!"

Unfortunately, it's not likely that anyone has spoken to her in such a way. The mirrors she likes to stop in front of are satisfactory but silent. And time is brief and nimble. Annette has some superficial practice in tidying up. The washstand takes her five minutes, the bed three, the table two. Gentlemen like to leave their suits draped over chair backs. That creates complications. In addition there are papers, books, letters on the desk. The hotel rules forbid meddling with guests' informal arrangements. But the room still needs to be cleaned. Each piece of paper has to stay where it is. That can take up to twenty minutes! Then she has to supervise her girls. They're such chatterboxes, the signals go off, green and persistent, and they simply ignore them. Annette has to bring them up to the mark. She works from twelve noon to nine at night. One hour off for lunch. Downstairs, next to the kitchen, at the long staff table that reminds you of mealtimes in an orphanage. If Annette goes on working so hard, she will surely make it to housekeeper herself—and will be able to go on working.

One day, a Wednesday, I ran into her outside one of the big cinemas. She was looking at the stills, scenes from a rich background. (Nothing is so interesting to the poor as the lives of the rich.) I permitted myself, since we had known each other for so long, to treat her. We saw one of those films that pass for "socially conscious". One of those films in which a well-off young man persistently tries to take a poor girl to supper, when she doesn't know whether you eat ice-cream with a fork, or use a nutcracker on an apple. The audience of course knows, and brays its approval to the film industry. At least on that evening, it was braying. Madame Annette said:

"Don't you think that girl might have learned a thing or two from films? Surely she'll have been to the cinema, seeing as the film is set in New York."

Thereupon—from a slightly hasty, slightly honest reaction against the whole business—I asked Madame Annette to accompany me to dinner in a good restaurant. Here and there sat a guest from the hotel. Here and there an appraising look brushed Madame Annette, not a recognizing one—because a real gentleman never imagines a chambermaid could be sitting in the same restaurant as himself. *En passant*, I make mention of the fact that Madame Annette was wearing a dark high-necked dress that made her look pale, and her mouth even redder—and a string of artificial pearls that threw a silvery-blue reflection on the lower half of her yellow-brown face. What seems more important to me is to stress that she handled her cutlery better than those men in the film industry with whom I have had occasion to eat, or as they like to say, to "dine".

Frankfurter Zeitung, 9 February 1929

44

The *Patron*

(1929)

I t is among the characteristics of the hotel manager that it's not possible to tell his age. The observer is mystified to see a fifty-year-old hotel manager at eleven in the morning, who by three o'clock will be a dashing forty, and late at night, fifty again, as he was in the morning. Not as rapidly as his physiognomy, but still remarkably fast are the changes in his hair and beard. There are times when little threads of silver seem to infiltrate his coal-black moustache. A couple of days later they are gone. Sometimes one seems to catch the hair on his head beginning to thin. Then a day or two later, there it is again, in all its familiar silky, almost feminine abundance.

Even though he is the utterly cosmopolitan manager of an utterly cosmopolitan hotel, the staff only ever refers to him as *le patron*. Maybe it's a challenge to the poor employees, even though they spend their whole lifetimes in the vicinity of modern capital, to conceive of a publicly owned company as their bread-giver, to serve an abstract notion sprung from thin ribbons of tickertape; and to see the man who hires and fires them, who orders them to do one thing and forbids them to do something else, merely as the employee of a mysterious joint-stock company. It's simpler to take him for a *"patron"*. If he were the actual owner, yes, even if he were only a shareholder, then—that's my sense of him—he surely wouldn't stand for the populist, provincial, and faintly demeaning title of "*patron*". But as things stand, the director is quite pleased, even a little flattered, to be addressed as "*patron*".

Such secrets of his soul as I sometimes think I can guess at, along with other, more evident traits of his, have long kept me from warming to the director as I would have liked. Writerly objectivity demands a certain sympathy for the person one describes, a literary sympathy, that in certain circumstances can even be expended on a louse. But my private heart beats in a sentimental (and now rather unfashionable) way for the lesser beings who are given orders and who obey, obey, obey, and rarely allows me to feel anything but objectivity for the others who order, order, order. As far as the director is concerned, then, I sometimes repeat the extenuating circumstance: he too receives orders; only from his shareholders! But the orders he receives are given him once a year, and they hold good for all 365 days, they are general instructions, written down on thick paper, almost like official documents. He can impart them to those below as he thinks fit, and if they seem harsh, as often, he can make them still harsher, which does something to make his own lot seem easier to him by comparison. Insofar as the ladder leading up to the company board is visible, then he, the director, is on its topmost rung.

Even so, I would long have become reconciled to all this, were it not among his habits to appear very quietly in unexpected places. Suddenly he appears in a remote part of a corridor. He looks as though he's been standing there for ever, and only started moving when he heard my approach. Another time there he is, striding through the lobby with lowered head, as though to indicate that he has no interest in anyone. But I know well that his eyes, which are set wide apart by the temples, like a bird's or a lizard's, swiftly and reliably take in the scenes around him, and that a short stroll is enough for the director to know who is in the lobby, what the porter's up to, and whether all the liftboys and errand boys are present. His glance hooks itself into the scene like a harpoon. He could as well take it back to his office to have it developed or stuck in an album.

He has the habits, movements and gifts of a detective. Born in the Levant to Greek parents, he has the quick-wittedness one ascribes to Greeks and Levantines. What he opens his eyes on he sees, and what he sees he understands. He is fluent in very many languages. There is not one in which he can write an error-free letter. He dictates a few key points to his secretary, probably sensible ones; he leaves the details to her. Of average height, though thin enough to make him appear much taller, he looks like a noble example of a very distant and very alien race. In his dark brown, narrow and seemingly planed-off face, the hooked nose stands out like a weapon, a curved skin and bone dagger. The right half of the narrow brow is covered by a wave of black hair. The trimmed moustache is curved like a black wire—it is shaved above and below—seeming to lie in the middle of the long upper lip. He rarely opens his mouth, not even to speak. If he had no teeth, one wouldn't know it.

Without question, the man has the imagination to produce and cater for so-called "luxury". If there is any creature that knows what "comfort" means, then it is the *patron*. All the details of décor speak for him. Throughout the hotel there are no high-edged tables that make your arm go to sleep when you rest it on them. The bedside lamps are comfortably within reach on adjustable boards in little safe-like niches. You don't lie in bed, afraid to reach for a glass of water for fear of knocking over the lamp. The ashtrays are all deep, wide and heavy. Every bed is curtained off, so as to be discreetly out of sight in the daytime. Framed by the two doors that lead out into the corridor, the room is large enough for the room-service waiter to be able to leave a small table out with your order, in case he is not able to enter the room. Along with the post, the guest is brought a selection of newspapers from various countries. Never is a mailman allowed to come up with registered mail without being telephoned through. All night, the so-called "pantry" is kept open, for orders of fruit, sandwiches, tea, coffee, and brandy. The large revolving door is open all night, so that you never need to ring the bell and waken the night porter. At three in the morning, there are as many lights on as there are at nine at night. All these details pay tribute to the director.

And yet the way he instructs a liftboy to follow him to his office is embarrassing to me. He doesn't say: Come with me! Nor does he wave at him or glance at him. He stops in front of the unhappy boy, looks at him, takes a step away, and turns round. I don't know what goes on behind the office door. But I can see employees as they come out. They straighten their tunics, swivel their heads in their collars as though to straighten their vertebrae, and give themselves a little shake, before going back on duty, as though they were emerging from a different world and needed a little time to adjust. Even if they weren't gone for any more than ten minutes! You could ask them a question—they wouldn't hear you. Their ears are still booming with a terrible noise that drowns out every subsequent sound.

It may be that this is only natural, and comes with the territory. But what is unnatural is his way of always uttering the same banalities and asking unanswerable questions. "Have you come from very far away? Did you have a good time? Pleasure to see you again, really, a great pleasure!" And, according to the weather and the season: "Dull old day, isn't it! It looks like rain!" Or: "Lovely, clear autumn we're having. It's the best thing for you. Have a nice day." And concluding with a bow that turns his body into a question mark: "The hotel safe's always at your disposal! Goodbye!"

And yet I once witnessed the following scene:

At about ten in the morning, a man came through the revolving door into the lobby. The director was just standing in front of the door of the reception clerk and was about to be on his way. The poor man stopped in the middle of the lobby, as though someone had left him there and forgotten all about him. His raincoat was flapping around him. His stumpy red hands looked like stockings. His face was bony, but clean-shaven and bleeding. The thin neck wobbled about in the stiff collar that was far too big for it. A little below, one sensed the presence of (but did not see) a soft, striped, not terribly clean shirt.

The director said to the man: "Get out, and come back through the goods entrance."

The man did so. He stepped out as though from a stage set. His behaviour was a little theatrical as it was. He took a rubber band off a letter case, and pulled out a few papers.

The director instructed the man to unfold them. He didn't move to take them from him, merely gave them one of his cursory glances. Then he shook his head.

The poor man went off. Then the director quietly said: "Psst!"

The man turned round.

"Come to lunch, today, twelve-thirty sharp!"

The poor man smiled and tried a sort of curtsey. Then he walked off.

"Psst!" said the director quietly, a second time.

The poor man turned round again, quicker and more trustfully than the last time.

And the director said to the porter: "Get him a coffee with milk!" and walked off. In mid-step he stopped again and called out over his shoulder, without turning:

"On second thoughts, make that cream!"

And he vanished into his office.

It wasn't enough to persuade me that he was a good man. But I have at least attained the necessary literary objectivity towards the *patron*.

Frankfurter Zeitung, 20 February 1929

45

Leaving the Hotel
(1929)

I would like to have caught up with some of my other friends at the hotel, but I am leaving tomorrow. I have been here for long enough. If I stayed longer I would be unworthy of the great blessing of being a stranger. I might degrade the hotel to a home if I no longer left it unless I had to. I want to feel welcome here, but not at home. I want to be able to come and go. I prefer to know that a hotel is waiting for me here. I am aware that this too is a sentimentality, and that, out of fear of a more conventional one, I am falling for one of my own devising. But that's the human heart for you.

I will let the chief receptionist know that I am leaving. Oh, not because of any regulations! This hotel pins no "avisos" in its rooms, no "extract from the hospitality and innkeeping bye laws of 1891, Article. IV §§ 18 and 22 ff.", no house rules and nowhere a "Guests are requested to inform the front desk of their departure in a timely fashion, so as to avoid being billed for a further night. Respectfully, The Management." No, this hotel pins no commandments on its walls. Nor does the fact that there is a restaurant on the premises require special mention, seeing that the restaurant is a good one, and people like to eat there. If I choose to inform the receptionist of my departure today, then it's purely because I need his kindness, and because I want to hear him murmur: "Oh dear, so soon!?" —

Such a tone! It's said so quietly, like a secret; as though my decision might be put off, so long as it's just the two of us who know about it ... It's as slow and protracted as a long-running lament. It seems to issue from that indescribable distance to which I now propose to go. The good fellow! — How will he manage without me? Whom will he say goodnight to when he goes home at night in his smart suit? How well we understood one another. We conversed with looks and glances, in the truly international language of stenoscopy! Which is now at an end ...

But men need to be tough, and so the chief receptionist asks me which train or ship I am proposing to leave on. I merely give him my destination and an approximate time, say, "evening". And he comes back with: what about train No. 743 with wagons-lits, leaving at 6.32 p.m., two stops, dining car until 10 p.m.? Backed up by a series of further suggestions. I leave the choice with him. It's among the virtues of a good receptionist to separate the best trains from those less good, even though he rarely goes anywhere himself, and his guests constantly. I am happy to rely on him. And if the train he has recommended should happen to arrive three hours late, then I am convinced that all the others will have been derailed. Such luridness, when all I wanted was to be comforted ...

Tomorrow will be the longest day. I have, to all intents and purposes, left, but not gone. Word has got out. The room-service waiter, who goes off shift in the afternoon, wished me *bon voyage* in the morning. He will have said it with one eye on his tip, but that doesn't make him any less sincere. The sincerest good wishes are those of people who are getting a tip. Whoever doesn't stand to get anything from me wishes me to the devil. Lucky the man therefore who can afford to leave a tip! The good people will bless him, because they hope he will be back soon. It's instructive to see that the waiter does me the honour of esteeming my generosity and my little gift at the same time. He likes me as much as he likes my money. (My friends all prefer my money.) And in his look I can distinguish between the sparkle of joy and a shimmer of melancholy. In his joy at his takings is mixed a little sorrow at parting. Well, goodbye!

It will be the longest day. It's as well that the room contains nothing, not one item that would seek to attach my eye painfully to itself. No quaint sugar box, no great-uncle's writing-desk, no maternal grandmother's portrait, no basin decorated with red flowers and a little crack, no familiar creaking floorboard that one suddenly falls in love with because one is about to leave, no mouth-watering smells issuing from the kitchen, and no brass ornamental pestle and mortar on the hall dresser. — Nothing. When my suitcases are gone, others will take their place. When my soap is packed away, someone else's will nestle by the basin. When I am no longer standing by the window, someone else will be. This room doesn't seek to deceive itself or you or me or anyone. By the time I look round it one last time before I go, it will already have ceased to be my room. The day is so long because there is no melancholy to fill it.

I don't need to pay any farewell calls in this city. I'm happy to think that the old man doesn't live here who hates me and whom I hate, and whom I keep having to say hello to. Nor even a younger man who is all of a heap when he sees me still alive, and who would be offended if he didn't see me. Nor is there my dear friend who walks me to the station and even as we shake hands for the last time remains convinced that he is doing worse out of our friendship than me. There is not even a lady with whom (out of gallantry) I am in love, and who, even as her eye blinks back a tear, is already happy that another man has looked her up and down. I am a stranger in this town. That's why I was so at home here.

There will be only one brief sentimental moment: when the porter has stowed away my suitcases and is standing on the platform, cap in hand, and his other hand under his apron, for fear lest it should involuntarily extend itself. Because it's quite a complicated business, this tipping. He takes it quickly, but clumsily. It's almost like a form of handshake, swift, and a little bungled. Then he takes a couple of steps back, the old fellow, still facing me. He puts his cap back on. One last time the letters that spell the dear name of the hotel flash at me.

Then I hoist sails, and board my train.

Frankfurter Zeitung, 24 February 1929

46

The Hotel

(1930)

The lobby is brightening with a specifically hotel morning. The broad mirroring glass is already variegated with the grey of the day ahead, while a few lamps hang from the ceiling like isolated stars. It's as though their tardy gleam is bound up with the presence of the night porter who switched them on the night before. They are his lights. When he leaves they will pale, and the day will break.

Sturdy cleaning women are moving about like huge, blue-aproned monsters on the stripped marble of the formal staircase; on the landing, where a plaster cherub has been spewing water into a precious basin for eternities, and an ancient palm gives unnecessary shade, leans a glistening bundle of brass stair rods, newly polished, a little heap of rays or weapons. With flying tails, the early waiters circumnavigate the blue-aproned monsters, discreetly steaming trays on their splayed hands. From backward corridors where it is still completely night-time drones the indefatigable song of the vacuum. Like a patient storm it wanders like an all-flattening fury over the maroon carpets. Just now the head waiter enters the hotel. He is wearing a mouse grey coat and green hat and looks like a forester. But just wait. The modest rustic garb covers the festive gleam of his tails. Soon you will see that he resembles a servant or a marquis in an old comedy. With a

magnificent gesture, like someone drawing a pair of gorgeous curtains he throws open the lofty doors to the breakfast room. It's as
though the day had lurked all night in the breakfast room, perhaps
been shut in there overnight, and only now were allowed to dawn
in the lobby and the rest of the hotel. All at once the blue cleaning women, the phantoms of early morning, are gone. Suddenly
the lamps, the tardy stars, are extinguished. Suddenly, his fair face
dusted with shaving powder, there stands the chief receptionist in
his eyrie. The night porter is already swallowed by his bed.
Suddenly the maroon carpets lie snugly over the formal staircase,
and it's as though morning in person is coming down the stairs.
The elevator hums. The first breakfast guests appear. Elderly
ladies and gentlemen who don't sleep much and who therefore
have made it a healthful habit to rise early. Taut, with a determined
show of opposition to their own years, looking neither left nor
right, they step out in the direction of the breakfast room, like
groups come together for a procession or coronation; each one his
own morning. Day is at hand.

The old people are still at breakfast when the young ones come
down. The lawful couples are not to be distinguished from the
unlawful ones. Both have in common the successfully overcome
night. Breakfast together is like an asseveration of their love. They
eat as though they had been eating together for decades, but the
head waiter knows what's what. They don't prod at doubtful eggs.
They drink their coffee lukewarm. The night just past hovers over
them, and the one ahead moves into view. The young man ignores
his newspaper. Anyone who has no eyes for the newspaper is young
and in love.

In the afternoon there is the "five o'clock tea". The potted palms
seem to have reproduced. Thanks to them the tropical climate of
the Negro dances (supported also by the central heating) becomes
a wholly successful illusion. At tiny miniature tables, with tiny
miniature coffee cups resembling thimbles, sit corpulent ladies who

have been prescribed Marienbad, trying to keep their movements refined, while their daughters, with less need to be careful, let themselves fall into the arms of gigolos. Stirred by the gentle breeze of so many passing waiters, the leathery leaves of the palms distribute heat and cool at once, and even though there is no short-age of noise, their gentle clicking becomes a sort of sonorous silence. Every noise that is created here has a component of silence as well, and every sound is so discreet that all the sounds put together make up the soul of discretion. Minor disturbances seem to apologize for themselves, even as they happen. — Serious men foregather in the conference room, far from the music. To look at them, you would think they were deciding the fate of the world, here, in a spare half hour between first-class trains. They determine our prices, our wages, and the degree of our hunger. Impossible to understand the things they say. Because they are speaking in one place, it is possible to dance in another. That's all. They are not speaking in spite of the dancing in the other room. No, they speak here so that there may be music and the world can continue on its merry way. All wheels will grind to a halt when their grim word says so.

And then the night porter comes along, and lights the evening. Fresh, youthful, shaved and powdered, in blue and gold livery, he rises like a second morning when the world has evening. Trains have arrived from exotic parts, and exotic visitors are wafting through the glass wings of the revolving doors into the lobby. Those who have been here for a day already and are sitting in the lobby, they are no longer strangers. No, they are long-established, the maroon carpets are their turf which they will not leave, and they cast slighting, suspicious looks at the new arrivals. The suit-cases pile up in front of the reception desk, plastered with labels from hotels in foreign places, Venice, Merano, Buenos Aires and San Francisco, all trying to legitimate these new guests. The head waiter surfaces for a moment to assess who can afford to buy themselves a meal under the palms (breakfast, of course, is *compris*). Sceptically, in spite of himself, he turns to face again the familiar meals, his friendliness is put together from understanding of the world, his faith in humanity is lined with suspicion, his cheery optimism is his pessimism turned inside out, when he smiles he is crying somewhere about the poverty of this world.

Before long, in about two hours, he will put on his little green hat and slip into his mouse grey coat, and with grand gestures he will shut the dining room—and then, in a corner, go over the accounts with the waiters, an accountant himself now, no longer a maître d'hôtel, a plain forester from the hunting grounds of reality. He will say a hurried goodnight to the night porter, whose day is now beginning. Already fresh stars are glimmering in the lobby's pale sky.

Frankfurter Zeitung, 23 November 1930

Part VII

Pleasures and Pains

Spring

(1921)

I am woken by the sound of carpets being beaten overhead. The muffled thudding provokes my neighbour's canary, and he cheeps and twitters and warbles like a bird song imitator. In the yard a window flies open, a second, a third: the whole building seems to be tearing off its windows.

A ray of sunshine splashes in my violet inkwell. The bronze maiden on my desk protects her bosoms from the intrusive beam and sweetly tans.

A hurdy-gurdy is playing in the yard. The streams of melody burst through, melting and freed.

From these and other signs, one notices eventually that it's spring.

On Kurfürstendamm the cafés put out spring awnings, the ladies have new wardrobes, the gentlemen natty yellow twittering gloves. In side streets the children play with shiny buttons and marbles. The blue-bedizened sky checks its reflection in the brass shaving bowl outside the barber's shop.

Everyone is freshly varnished and "please don't touch". Slips of girls wander about on the asphalt in sheer stockings and new boots looking like costumed willow trees.

In the afternoon I sit in the window and think that Sunday is on its way. To Grunewald, for instance.

After six or still later, a girl in purple rings the doorbell. Love is like that.

Freie Deutsche Bühne, 16 June 1921

People in Glass Cages
(1922)

I t is the time of year when a yen for freedom cruelly evicts bundled-up individuals from their cosy flats and into their brazen winter gardens.

In the morning a sunbeam or streak of rain strikes a coffee cup. And in the evening a traffic light bleeds to death.

Turned out and visible to all, the bosom of the family, with whatever had kept it hidden all winter. Intimate gestures are enacted in full sight of the prying neighbours.

Lips explode in kisses clattering along the streets, and forks drop from the hands of unfettered paterfamiliases with a whimpering jingle.

Walls have eyes. Man is in a glass cage, shown for what he is in helplessness, rage and shirtsleeves, barely concealed by the odd flower pot. He hangs suspended over the pavement like his own canary.

Dew anoints a nose sniffing the clouds, and a chill evening wind brushes a hairy chest, swelling the tourist's shirt like a sail.

A sultry haze of aired bedding and other matters fights down the shy scent of a debatably flowering lilac. Oh, the struggle to lead a useful life weighed down by nappies in a rear courtyard!

Das Blaue Heft, 8 July 1922

People on Sunday
(1921)

On Sundays the world is as bright and empty as a balloon. Girls in white dresses wander about the streets like so many church bells, all smelling of jasmine, sex and starch.

The sky is invariably freshly painted. The buildings swim in sunshine, and the towers scramble nimbly upwards. At the edge of the city Nature takes over, as one can tell by the proliferation of Do Not signs. It is mostly green, and consists of postcard views tacked together.

Nature is particularly important on Sundays. Basically, Sunday has been instituted for the sake of nature. All the communications disrupted on weekdays between nature and humanity are restored on Sunday. In fact, Sunday is the bridge to the forgotten and discarded Holies of the world: such things as woods, the Wannsee, the Luna Park and the Almighty.

People ring in Sundays with bells, the beating of carpets, and indolent coffee in bed. They throw open their windows and sniff freedom. They ransack wardrobes and chests of drawers and put on special items to celebrate the day of idleness on which their souls dangle.

On Sunday I stand by the window. The house opposite has thrown open all its windows like glass butterfly wings as though— whoosh, didn't you see it!?—to fly away. It can't, though, it is too weighed down by furniture, people and destinies.

Which have changed as well: my neighbour, a double-entry bookkeeper only yesterday (at the same firm for twenty-five years "without a bonus")—and today, not even a single entry. With God in his heart and the taste of coffee still in his mouth, he hurries over to the window in his shirtsleeves to fill his lungs with a draft of freedom.

When I see him in the week in his threadbare jacket his hands are dangling from his sleeves as though the fingers were a frayed part of the jacket; now he looks to me like the hero of a story, or several stories.* He could, I am thinking, be offered a much better-paid job, but he is unable to resign. Perhaps he even stood once or twice outside his boss's double doors, and his courage was quelled, as the movements outside the double door are quelled, and his heart resembled a squishy cushion, one of those plump leather cushions a manager likes to sit on.

One Monday morning, after he's stuffed himself full of courage the whole of the day before, he went to work, and the boss walked in and presented him with some trifling thing, maybe a fountain pen, or an inkwell, and the employees put flowers on his desk, because that Monday marked the twenty-fifth anniversary of his entry into the firm, and he had forgotten about it. And so now he can't resign.

I think I am going to call him Gabriel.

Today, Sunday, Gabriel will set his gramophone on the table in front of him. And a Caruso record put together from shellac and warble will pour over Gabriel the chant and melody of an unfamiliar world where figures and steel nibs are unknown.

Canaries like to mark Sundays as well. In the first-floor window is the bird cage and the canary recites an Eichendorff ode. Or maybe it's something by Baumbach.

On the red tablecloth rests a white crocheted doily. The children

* See J.R.'s 1920 story "Career" in his *Collected Shorter Fiction*.

can't be dissuaded from propping their elbows on it, and rucking it up.

I have never seen the mother except in a blue dressing gown. She is very quiet, I think she was born in slippers, and I'm sure she has a shuffling and embittered soul.

She scolds the children for rucking up the tablecloth. What does she have to have a tablecloth for, I wonder, and once I sent her a couple of drawing pins in a matchbox, with instructions for their use. But she went on chastising the children.

Today, on Sunday, though, she had cake for them. The children rucked up the tablecloth, but their mother stood in the window and took delight in the declamations of the canary. She had on a white blouse. And no trace of any slippers.

But Sunday evenings are sad. I see the tabby cat sitting on the third-floor window sill. The teacher has gone out.

Each time the clock sends a quarter hour ringing out over the copper roofs of the town, the cat stretches. I suspect that she is keeping count of the strokes, and is impatient for her mistress to come home.

Sometimes she looks down, and for want of a handkerchief, waves with her tail when she sees the teacher coming.

The teacher has gone to visit her brother, who is a retired infantry captain with hearing loss. It takes her for ever to tell him there is no news. That's what has caused the teacher to be gone such a long time.

"I swear I'm going to sack her!" says the cat, and is terribly agitated.

Sunday evenings are thin and mealy, as if they already belonged to Monday. Gabriel is back to being a double-entry bookkeeper, and the girls iron their creased white dresses and smell of bread and butter. The world is full again.

Berliner Börsen-Courier, 3 July 1921

50

The Office
(1924)

Because I am going abroad, I am required to call on various offices, many offices, grey buildings, grey-white rooms, gentlemen at desks, gentlemen behind counters, gentlemen in worn suits, with embittered faces, with moustaches and bald heads, with widening partings and spectacles, with blue pencils in their top pockets—wretched men, wretched offices. There is no more than a partition between us, but it is a whole world. I lean against desks and see red, blue, purple inkpads and hammer-headed rubber stamps, chewed-up pens, toothmarks sunk in brown pencils, old pictures, office calendars with the frayed remnants of old, torn-off days, scraps of paper in tin frames, gnawed by the tooth of time which eats a date for breakfast every morning. I pass through corridors, unreal, almost dream-like corridors, past waiting people propped on umbrellas reading newspapers. Sometimes a door opens, and I steal a look inside and see a man sitting, a desk standing, a calendar hanging, just as in the room I will shortly set foot in, even though the one carries the number twenty-four, and mine is sixty-four. A couple of flies bombard the windowpanes, hurling their little black bodies against the glass, while a third stands on the tin lid of the inkwell rubbing its nose with its frail legs. The ink in the inkwell is drying, crusts are forming round the edges, blue-black crusts, dried, prematurely wizened figures, reminders, files.

At the front desk sits a young man and at the back desk an older man. The young man has white-blond hair, which is nice and unruly, it objects to being parted, and then he has a blobby round nose and a red Cupid's bow and a dimpled chin like a girl. There is the child in his face still, his blue eye is earnest and adorable like a boy's playing cops and robbers. His hands have dumpy shapeless fingers, and one of them is already wearing a wedding band. His waistcoat is gently swelling over the beginnings of a pot belly, emblem of his career. His briefcase is still new, the fair hands of a young wife have stuffed it full of sandwiches, a sleepy morning tenderness still clings to his lips, and he is friendly, gentle, fair, he makes a modest joke in order to encourage me, the "pending case", to a light-hearted rejoinder. He is the man on the other side of the barrier. The sunken wall, the partition dividing us, is shattered; with the longing of a man on a desert island he looks up at me, heart overflowing with gratitude. He is like the stationmaster who sees the express race past him every day without stopping—and I am just as exotic here, just as strange and mysterious as the train that never stops. This young official would like to detain me, he wants to know what it's like in those countries I have visited, and where I hope to go. He wants to know about more than the countries. He is young, he longs for human conversation, he takes an interest in me, he is still unhappy at his desk, not yet chewing his pencils, he too has bold dreams. He still has the sacred faith in the impossible, he is determined to one day leave this room, to have money, to sit in express trains, to see Mt Fuji for himself. But when I come back to this office in twenty years' time, then he will be the older gentleman at the back desk who will give me a doubtful look over the top of his bifocals, an elderly gentleman with a bald patch and the dry skin coming off it in little flakes. Fresh ink will have crusted around the edges of the inkwell, the two hundredth generation of flies will be assaulting the windows. And my friend, I fear, will be chewing pencils.

Prager Tagblatt, 20 July 1924

51

The Destruction of a Café

(1927)

The café was as old as a church.

Stout pillars supported the ceiling, which seemed to disappear in the gloaming. It was flat, and covered with paintings. But because it was propped by pillars, and grey cigar smoke clouded it, you couldn't help feeling that it was vaulted, that you had arches overhead that sheltered but also swaddled you, a roof and also a robe.

The pillars were dark brown, and a polished bark covered them, as if they had reverted to the status of trees. At eye-level they put out iron hooks, decorated by iron foliage. The tables stood in their shade. One knew the size of the pillars, where each one began and ended; but measured with that measure that has no units, but is nevertheless real and true, the pillars were endless, and whoever leaned on one was alone, as alone as in a room by himself. Someone else might be resting against the other side of the pillar. But he was a hundred years away. The din of conversation was muffled by the coats that hung on the hooks, trapping indiscretions in their folds. It was possible to sit in the middle of the café, and yet remain as concealed as in the middle of a forest.

To enter the café, you had to push aside a heavy green velvet curtain with leather trim. It was heavier and fitted more snugly than a door of iron or oak. It was draped around the shoulders of the entry, like a winter cloak. You batted it aside, walked in, and straightaway it closed behind you. You were in the warm—whether it was autumn or February or even Christmas.

Across from the entrance on a raised platform was the wide dark bar. Looming in the background were innumerable bottles of various shapes and sizes, colourful gold-rimmed labels, and in front of them a regiment of gleaming glasses, opalescent cups and a jingling, singing heap of frivolous teaspoons—a lady sat or stood behind the bar. One couldn't see quite where she was rooted. Her growth was a mystery. It was possible that she perched on a bar stool. Her complexion was pale, a little subterranean, as though lit by ancient candles. The outline of her face was fine—her face was little more than outline—she reminded one of a well-preserved spring. Perhaps she didn't exist at all, and someone had sketched her with fawn crayon on soft paper. Because it was as though she was looking out of a frame, or from a high window over rooftops. Her eye strayed, without aim …

A mannerly gentleman made his way quietly through the room. He knew all the customers. He would suddenly pop up behind a pillar to help someone into his coat, he had clearly been following the man's movements for some time—and now there he was, at the right time. He offered a restrained greeting with the dignity of someone who has been greeted himself with considerably less warmth over decades. — Good evening—his inclined head seemed to say—no need to thank me. I don't need thanks. — As he held out the coat, he seemed to turn into a hat stand with extended arms. If a waiter was negligent, the gentleman got his attention with a long look. Like a general he surveyed the terrain, like a doctor he offered diagnoses, like the master of a house he welcomed visitors, like a theatre director he supervised the waiters' entrances and exits, like a protective angel he watched over the forsaken and alone, and like God he was unchanging. He was neither young nor old, his hair was neither white nor dark, his expression was neither animated nor listless, and never did I see him sit and rest.

This was the café where my friend Krac would come in the evenings, with books and manuscripts, the evening paper, and a roll (filled). Other people would go home at this time, or out to dinner, but he, *secum portans*, liked to eat his supper here. He held it under the table in his left hand, and with his right helped himself to little unexplained titbits. Other people would take a couple of soft-boiled eggs in a glass, reddish-yellow, with scraps of shell mixed in. He for his part would order a cup of coffee, not even an espresso, just a common or garden coffee. The whole of the café where we sat, the table, the chairs, the pillar behind us, the waiter, the mannerly gentleman, the lights, the bar and the lady were like condiments for my friend's roll. Meanwhile the café was happy to act as though it had requested him to come, bringing his supper. Such was the hospitality of this institution.

It's not so easy any more.

The café has been redecorated. There is no longer a curtain in the entrance. To keep the pillars clear, a wardrobe has been installed to the right of the door. You are supposed to surrender your coat when you walk in, as at the theatre. The large windows have narrow green sills. The pillars are white, the ceiling is white. Away with the wall-paintings!—said the spirit of the age—the smoke obscures them anyway. The colour of the age is white, laboratory white, as white as the room where they invented lewisite, white as a church, white as a bathroom, white as a dissecting room, white as steel and white as chalk, white as hygiene, white as a butcher's apron, white as an operating table, white as death, and white as the age's fear of death! Let's brighten up the ceiling! — Because it is the age's belief that white is cheerful. It wants by brightness to attract cheerful people. And the people are as merry as patients, and the present is as merry as a hospital.

The ceiling hasn't been lowered, it's sufficient to have had it painted white. Now it presses down on our heads, unremitttingly hygienic. Light is cast not by lamps, but by glass columns that

resemble thermometers—perhaps they take the room's temperature at the same time. Light streams in from the side, not harmful
to the eyes, so that blind people with artificial eyes can read *faits
divers*. The floor is no longer wood, but grey stone marked with
white lines—or so it appears. (Your feet tell you that the stone is
actually rubber or linoleum.) A cowardly stone that makes no
sound, a stone for tiptoeing around on. Hygienic. Deaf-mutes can
listen to the radio in this silence. The number of tables has been
increased by a third, and the comfortable armchairs have been
thrown out. The new chairs are straight-backed for straight backs,
they steel the body, they are steel seats. The bar looks like the
counter of a pharmacy. The waiter has a prescription pad. A boy
with gold buttons, a milk and blood face, bum-freezer jacket,
Cupid, Mercury and messenger-boy in one, doles out nicotine-free
cigarettes. On special application you are served coffee that will
cure heart-patients and put you to sleep. The lady behind the bar
is gone, vanished, airbrushed out, removed. The mannerly gentleman is gone. (Will you ever be greeted like that again?) He couldn't
go along with the evolution of the café, the way that claims to go
from Germany to Broadway, but never gets past Kurfürstendamm.

Frankfurter Zeitung, 21 October 1927

52

Music in the Volksgarten
(1928)

The music in the Volksgarten began at five in the afternoon. It was spring, and the blackbirds were still warbling in the shrubbery and the flowerbeds. The army band was seated behind the gold-tipped iron railings that separated the restaurant terrace from the park concourse, and thus parted the paying guests from other listeners without means. Among these were many young women. They had come to enjoy the music. But music on those evenings meant more than music, it was a chance to hear the voice of nature and of spring. The leaves overarched the proud melancholy of the trumpets—and a fitful breeze seemed for long moments at a time to whisk away the whole band and all the noises on the terrace to unknown distances. At the same time, one could hear the slow, crunching footfall of walkers on the footpath. Their settled tempo gave back the pleasure the music gave the ears. When the instruments sounded again, the drums began to roll, and the cymbals to clash, then it was as though the trees had grown louder, and the excitable arms of the bandleader had not only the musicians at his beck and call, but also the soughing leaves. Now, when suddenly a solo flute broke through the storm, it didn't sound like the voice of an instrument, but like a singing pause. Then the birds too resumed—as though the composer had written a part for blackbirds. The scent of the chestnuts was so strong that it drowned out the sweetest melodies, and it batted your face like a brother to the wind. And from the many young women in the avenue there came a lustre, and a whispering and in particular a laughter that was even closer than the women themselves, and more familiar. Then if you addressed a strange girl you thought you had already heard her speak. And if you went away with her from this avenue into another, more secluded, then you didn't have just the girl with you, you had something of the music, and you entered into the silence there as into one of the singing pauses.

It wasn't thought proper to lounge outside by the rails and let the girls know that you were in no position to go inside and order a coffee. And so I walked up and down the avenue, fell in love, despaired, got over it, forgot, and fell in love again—all in the space of a minute. I would have liked to stop and listen and nothing else. But even if I had been friends with a lieutenant who—all jingle and elegance—was sitting eating butter biscuits within, I would still have fallen for the distant and inaccessible charms of the lightsome ladies who sat at white garden tables, like so many spring clouds, impossible to speak to because one never saw them out on the streets anywhere. At that time, some of the "grand monde" would foregather on the restaurant terrace, and the barrier was the border that separated us. And just as the young lady I was kissing took me for a mighty knight, so on the terraces of the great restaurants I saw damsels I would straightaway have died for. I would get a chance later. But to be able to promenade up and down and discreetly watch life going on, and pretend it wasn't behind lock and key, that was something I owed myself.

From time to time I would spot a graceful ribbon that the silver-tipped conductor's baton of black lacquer had set spinning into the air. It hung there in my sight, a billowing memory. Sometimes, when I happened to be standing beside the exit, the seductive and supercilious look of a lady would brush me. She would get in a carriage, followed by a suite of gentlemen. But on the brief way from the threshold of the garden to the running board of the carriage, she demanded from my worshipful eye confirmation that she was beautiful. I fell in love instantly—meanwhile the carriage trundled off, and the dapper clopping of the horses mimicked my heart. I was still bewailing her disappearance, but already melancholy began to give way to the hope that the lady might leave the restaurant at the same time tomorrow, and I, a chance passer-by, would be on hand to see it and be noticed. And even though the music had recalled me to the avenue and the vulgar chancers, I was perfectly convinced that I was standing on the threshold of a magnificent existence that would begin tomorrow.

Already night had fallen, lamps came on among the leaves, and you couldn't see the young ladies any more, only hear them. In the dimness they seemed to have become more numerous. Giggling became their principal communication. Since I could no longer see their cheap blue dresses, the young ladies could almost compete with those within the enclosure. The public part of the garden was closing, and the band was getting ready to finish for the evening. One of the players went from desk to desk, gathering in the sheet music like so many school exercise books. The last piece—it was almost always the Radetzky March—wasn't played from the score, but from empty desks. The march seemed not to exist on paper. It had passed into the players' flesh and blood, and they were playing it from memory, as you breathe from memory. Now the march rang out—the Marseillaise of reaction—and while the drummers and trumpeters still stood at their places, you thought you could see the drums and trumpets march off by themselves, drawn along by the melody that poured from them. Yes, the entire Volksgarten was marching. People wanted to stroll and to dawdle, but the rolling drums got their limbs moving. They echoed long after in the street beyond, and suffused the noise of the evening city like a smiling and rapid thunder.

Frankfurter Zeitung, 8 April 1928

53

The Strange City
(1921)

For the past week, I've been living on a new street, and it feels like a different city. As yet I know little about the customs, population and dimensions of this city, but at least I have established its chief quality: it has balconies.

The man who built it was an architect with an obsession with the south. For twenty years his soul went about pregnant with gables and oriels and turrets and weathervanes, his soul was a sort of compressed version of Nuremberg, and then in the twenty-first it was let loose on some open space. And the architect gave expression to his dream of the south. Because this town was supposed to give a home to as many people as possible, he had to build large buildings, which meant setting one apartment over another and then another, till there were four or five squatting on top of each other. And then he dropped a pert Nuremberg gabled roof on top of the ensemble, and carved little balconies out of the bellies of the individual flats, and teased round and square bay-fronts out of the forms of the rooms. So that his yearning was satisfied, but only up at the top. The lower parts of the buildings have the usual facades, wide gateways, glass doors, tarnished door handles and zoological doorbells, for instance lions' heads with panting tongues you have to tickle to get the bell to ring. Along the corridors he set unframed mirrors. So that the people liked to go up—in the lift if they were well-off, taking the stairs if they weren't—and inspect themselves, though without getting to know themselves at all.

These buildings, which are still haunted by the architect's soul, make me indescribably sad, because they are so compromised. They were built for a purpose, which was to be habitable and durable, and full of light and air. But they aspired to be beautiful, and as impractical as beauty always is. They were forced to yield to the ridiculous duress of their physical being, and only in their upper reaches was it permitted to them to be luxurious, and even then under conditions of strict practicality. They symbolize the lives of thousands of architects, and the gulf between what they intended and what they actually built.

Some people like to say veran-dah. That sounds as though they had already fallen off them, with a flowerpot and half a window to follow. Because here everyone loves their veran-dah, and tricks it out with geraniums and begonias and pelargoniums, and other blooms that sounds like faraway countries. That comes from the longing of people who spend half their lives trying to set themselves apart from the rest of us, and the other half (in accordance with the proverb)* to create order. They may never get to anywhere with a name like one of their flowers. They plant these exotic things outside their houses and in their hearts, and so make the symbol of the thing-attained-with-difficulty domestic. In the same way their love of outdoors is best seen in brick promontories where they spend a great part of their lives, either with a watering can, or with love, appetite and illumination.

The light is dimmed to pink, and looks like a small-scale forest fire on the horizon, or a Light Everlasting in a wayside chapel somewhere. Now God has given me sufficient desire for beauty on the one hand to multiply the forest fires, and to quench them, and

---

* *Die Ordnung ist das halbe Leben*: order or organization is half of life.

also a devoutness that is susceptible to the occasional wayside chapel. But a whole parade of these wayside chapels, plastered on a row of trees, and animated by the earthly rattle of dinner-plates and clink of cutlery, is able to knock a sizeable hole in my spirit of reverence. So I sometimes direct an impious eye at the inner life of my neighbours, which they have turned inside out, to give it some air on their veran-dahs. On occasion I am ashamed of my over-weening mind and my secret shame, which prevents me from doing as my neighbours. I see isolated lights and I think of the wayside chapels. Maybe, I think, people would be more discreet and pious, if the essence of the veran-dah didn't consist in giving the illusion of being cast away on a desert island of swinging baskets. And the pinkish light—as I've discovered—is only another illusion. The one who sees it thinks he is not seen. And is seen, in the pink ... Perhaps people actually want to be seen.

One thing is certain: that I am all alone in this strange city, and that as I make my way through its streets, a shudder of homeless-ness will befall me one morning in the midst of so much homely activity. The energetic sound of a matutinal piano; the white net curtains behind a window; a man in shirtsleeves; a woman in her nightcap; a Litfass column dripping with fresh glue; a porter gone out to Brasso the doorknob; a spit-and-shined shoe-polish boy; a crisp lady baker; a hairdresser standing outside his premises like a white atomizer—they all are strange to me, because they don't know me, even though they tell me everything. They greet each other with familiar expressions, and every eye reflects the other's experiences.

People here are so clean. They smell of soap, those brown cubes of soap that my aunt used to use on me. The women here wear their hair straight back, exposing their ears. There's an atmosphere of spiritual chastening about them. Their hours overbrim with busy-ness, and their papers are all in order. They carry their souls in the palms of their hands. Their past is as stainless as the brass sink outside the barber's shop. Their pursuit is shopping. Their future is doing sums. They collect their days in an album, like so many stamps. They are collectors of days and years.

Never was anything mysterious in their lives, nor yet anything ugly. They grew and prospered in the shadow of their virtues.

How I envy them.

Every day I meet a gentleman on the stairs, who is by profession a representative.

I don't know what or whom he represents, but he's a representative. Even when he isn't wearing gloves, his hands are solemn, as though carrying mourning candles. He has a straw hat on, but I understand that it's really a topper. His stride is managerial. His eye rests heavily, punishingly on things. He is quiet, but I can hear the drone of his voice—a deep voice with thunderous aspects. I don't greet him, but it feels as though I did. Perhaps he is an undertaker, and is on his way to today's funeral.

He was a good and industrious son. Surely he was the apple of someone's eye once. I would sit down next to him in class, and unhesitatingly copy his answers.

I don't see his forehead, but it is certainly high and rounded. It must have room for the many solemn thresholds in his brain.

Sometimes I see him taking a blue-eyed girl by the hand, by the name of Lili. On those occasions he is *ex officio*. Once he bent down to her because she had lost her glove and it was as though an emperor had suddenly begun to laugh, or something human had happened to him.

I am getting to feel more at home in the strange city.

Berliner Börsen-Courier, 21 August 1921

54

Travel

(1921)

Guarded by customs inspectors and framed by passport regulations, abroad only starts to blossom beyond national frontiers; and that object of our desires called Far Away is only another jurisdiction with its own head of state and military, population statistics and tax regime. If you take an exotic sound for a cry of longing, it was probably nothing more than a locomotive's whistle. All the world's stations smell of anthracite rather than distant promise. The express train is muggy, stuffed with snoring well-set individuals who look nothing like travellers, are not redolent of mystery, but carry sandwiches in greaseproof paper, and exhibit all the frailties of their wretched humanity in the cramped compartment, sending the alarmed observer scuttling into the next one instead. Once, a beautiful damsel entered my compartment and my soul gave a lurch. The next morning, her eyes blinked open in the direction of the luggage rack, and I saw a creature in feminine apparel, her complexion ravaged by an agitated night with little sleep. The wind that came whistling through the open window mixed soot among her powder, and sleep had gummed up her eyelids. I dread to think what I looked like.

I entered another country, and pressed my ticket into the hands of a strange porter, instead of the visiting card I should have had. In the other city, I saw green copper cupolas and Gothic towers climbing into the sky. Beggars clustered outside church doors, stubble-faced lady beggars among them. They lay in wait for believers, and assaulted their impressionable souls with a litany of ills. Children, old people and women dropped coins in the laps of the beggars, thinking: God is my witness.

I looked into strange offices, and the desk-clerks who were working in them wore black sleeve-protectors, just as they do here at home. Blond and other variously dyed secretaries perched at typewriters, and pined for six o'clock, which is the hour of relief for the women of this century. It was a shade after two. A nearby clock rang the quarter-hour, and the girls pricked up their ears, hoping a miracle had taken place and they would hear it strike six. But just as obdurately as though it had been here at home it stuck to its assigned quarter past two, and the girls went back to their clacking. In other countries too, clocks are soulless pieces of machinery. And girls, increasingly, as well ...

I came to a hospital, and it too, like every other hospital in the world, smelled of camphor and iodine. The sisters fluttered from bed to bed in their white wimples like starched wings, and the patients groaned in such a familiar fashion, I had the sense I was at home. Evidently, so I thought, people only speak foreign languages when they are well. But pain is the greatest, all-conquering international movement there is, and truly its expression is as universal as music.

I visited the parks and gardens of the strange city too, those places where love flowered. Men and women came and went, and sat down together on benches, and assured one another of their feelings, which was unnecessary, because they were perfectly evident. Evening prowled along the footpaths, presumably waiting for night to fall. A constable plodded up and down, not noticing, even though he had a whole notebook for suspicious behaviour.

The people spoke differently. Their houses looked unfamiliar. (It was after all abroad.) But the representative things, the things that show the nation's face to the world, namely the border police and the customs inspectors—they are the same everywhere. They all have the same rapacious hands, and prying intrusive looks that feel like hands.

I have no idea what a man finds to say for himself after he's been abroad. I could sit at home for years on end, and be perfectly content. If only it weren't for the stations. You swear a shrill sound that pierces the night is just the whistle of a locomotive. It is a cry of longing. And every so often, exquisitely beautiful women walk into your compartment ...

Berliner Börsen-Courier, 2 *October* 1921

55

The "Romance" of Travel
(1926)

The joyful anticipation before a journey is always outweighed by the irritation of actually going. Nothing so irritating as a hulking station that looks like a monastery, at the sight of which I always wonder whether I shouldn't slip off my shoes, instead of hailing a porter. Nothing so irritating as an iron rail before a ticket office. In front of me hovers a rucksack. Behind me a pair of knitting needles pushed through the side of a basket stab me in the back. I need to practically bend double to tell the obtuse employee my destination. He has just one little window through which he takes in money and destinations. I am sure he would rather listen to my hands ...

All I know of the porter who has made off with my things is his number. I am dependant on his recollection of faces. What if he has none? What if some double of mine shows up? What if the porter has some kind of mishap? My friend needs a platform ticket if he is to see me off. What's the point of a platform ticket? The rails are off limits, and yet you pay to go on the platform. A man who sets foot on the platform in order *not* to travel, is doubly left behind. You might as well ask everyone in the whole station to have a ticket.

Next, there are the dauntingly high steps up to my carriage. Why not just have ladders? You clamber up into the carriage as into an attic to dry clothes. The compartments are like matchboxes sitting on one of their emery board sides. The seats are so parsimoniously designed that there is not an inch of space between my knees and those of the fellow opposite. We could set out a chess board on them. We can't open our eyes to look up—that would mean looking at the other. If we're really unlucky, then there are people either side of us as well. To take a cigarette out of our pockets we poke our neighbour in the ribs.

The so-called music of the wheels feels like hammer blows on my cerebellum and temples. If I stretch my leg, I involuntarily brush my neighbour's trousers. And we look at each other continuously: while cutting apples, eating sausages, peeling oranges. Of course we squirt juice into the other's eyes.

Our hands, our collars, our shirts, our handkerchiefs are blackened. The locomotive pours soot on my face. Often it takes us through so-called tunnels, which are the pride of modern engineering. We ride through the underworld, no coal-miners we. If we move to open a window, those with colds protest. If I leave the compartment I need to issue half a dozen excuse-me's first. The so-called communication cord is sealed. If you use it to communicate, you pay a fine. In case of a difference of views, the conductor's decision is final. Always to my disadvantage ...

If I should elect to go in a sleeping-car, that entails sharing a small cupboard with a large gentleman. A shared night is a night halved. (Passengers are segregated by sex, worse luck.) Wives require proof. If I eat lunch on board, plates, waiters and winebottles are all kept shaking in iron rings. Woe if they were set at liberty ... !

Conductors change about as often as April weather. They are there to draw lines on your ticket. Just lines. For that purpose, they like to wake me. These simple lines (sometimes perforations) I could do myself. Head-conductors like to check up on the lines left by the conductors. Lethally heavy suitcases teeter on luggage racks.

At the frontier, customs inspectors come on board, and help themselves to my cigars. In the corridors are framed axes and saws, forever hinting at the worst.

When you reach your destination, you fall over suitcases. If your suitcase is travelling separately, it entails waiting for it for an hour. All stations are built on a prodigal scale, but with very narrow exits to the world beyond. Tickets need to be surrendered. I wonder what the railways do with so much cardboard.

No one is so badly off as a traveller. It's a curious thing that this mediaeval torture of travelling should strike everyone as being so romantic. Our clothes are wrecked. We ruin our digestion with hot sausages and cold beers. We all have reddened eyes and dirty, greasy hands. And that should make us happy … !

Sometimes in films I see the saloon cars of American millionaires. They dictate business letters to typists. They sit in tubs and bathe, whilst travelling. A black valet rubs them dry. A cook prepares their favourite dish. Some travel in automobiles, which are independent of rails. A few take to the skies—capitalist birds. Why don't we demand these things? Our train tickets cost enough. We shouldn't have to pay for cinema seats as well.

Our so-called modes of transport lag far behind the times. They stand in no relation to the pride we take in our advanced civilization and the contempt we feel for post-chaises. Anyway, railway compartments are more like post-chaises than the railway authorities like to think. We're living in the wireless age, and still they like to punch holes in cardboard! The contemporaries of the dirigible balloon still lug their own suitcases! We are contemplating travelling to the moon. We are thinking about Mars. We have hit upon the Theory of Relativity. Just because we don't understand it doesn't mean we are happy to roost on chicken ladders when we have shelled out for beds.

Modern aeroplanes are more comfortable than trains. If I were of an aphoristic bent—which God knows I'm not—then I would say: It's better to crash by aeroplane than arrive by train. There are no para-chutes for train crashes. Nor have I seen life-jackets, come to that ...

Even doing fifty mph, you're still not travelling at the speed of time. Time passes at a hundred thousand miles per second. While I'm sitting in a speeding train, I'm still racing ahead of it. That's what the Theory of Relativity allows ...

I can transmit my likeness in an instant by telegraph. Transporting myself takes twelve hours. By the time I arrive, I'm no longer recognizable. You can't shave on a train. My beard grows faster than the train travels. You can't use the toilet at "station stops". While the train is moving it's continually occupied.

In third class you sit on wooden pallets, as in prison. If someone turns off the overhead lamp, there is no option but sleep all round. It's too dark to read the paper. When the light's on, the editorial jumps all over the place. You take the feuilleton page and bend it over your knee, just to prove it can be done.

If you put your head out of the window, you'll never see it again. It'll be in a well somewhere. If you lean against a door, you'll fly out like a piece of orange peel. And yet, it's forbidden to throw things out.

"All infractions are punishable." Luggage thieves "may be prosecuted". Not that you'll ever get your luggage back. Anyone supplying information leading to the conviction of a thief will be rewarded. But anyone who's ever tried will know how hard it is to get a reward from the railways.

On the contrary, there are often "supplementary fares" to be paid. (You even get given a receipt.) You can stick it in the mirror of the toilets—which are blind anyway.

Jumping onto a moving train is not allowed. Jumping off one is for criminals. In any case, ordinary humans are incapable of opening the door, unless, that is, they have the misfortune to lean against it accidentally while the train is in motion. Children must be kept on a leash. Dogs may not be taken at all. Meanwhile, chatty travellers are left criminally unmuzzled ...

There are luxury trains, expresses, local trains, various fees and classes, a forest of instructions, prohibitions, discouragements. All these are felt to be "romantic".

Even so, I would sooner travel to Monte Carlo first class than fill in a tax declaration on foot ...

Ed.: We assure our readers that in spite of everything he says about "romance", our author spends very little time at home.

Frankfurter Zeitung, 6 June 1926

56

The Lady in the Compartment
(1926)

A beautiful lady entered the compartment where I was reading the newspaper. She looked at my newspaper, not at me, told the porter to put up a large silver-studded leather case, sat down, and didn't have the right change. There was a long moment, filled with the silence of the porter, who was in a hurry. One could clearly feel the intensity with which the man was looking for an expression of impatience, haste, and possibly also bitterness. But seeing as he had no business looking impatient and embittered, he emanated a silence that was as pungent as any oath. At that moment I felt a great irritation with the beautiful lady. She was forcing me out of my tranquillity deepened by the enjoyment of the exciting newspaper to a painful pondering of how to find a swift and satisfactory solution to this predicament. Other men think on their feet, make remarks that win them the admiration of both ladies and porters. Whereas I was in the position that if I didn't quickly do something, I would be despised by the one, and laughed at by the other. I therefore asked: "What are you owed?"; was informed, gave the porter a tip that compelled him to thank me more loudly than I would have liked, and sat back to await developments. The lady, still hunting for change, came up with a big bill, and not looking at me, asked me whether I could change it for her. "No!" I said, and the lady looked some more. Her confusion must be very great; I resolved to take pity on her, but I couldn't do it, because I needed all my pity for myself. Was I to exclaim: "How delightful to be in credit with such a ravishing individual!" What a compliment! Was it not impertinent to disturb her in her search, was it not glib to seek to base an acquaintance on such a vulgar premise? I was unable to watch the lady, her hurried movements were of a private, even an intimate nature, and I thought I shouldn't stare at the contents and lining of her handbag.

But nor could I muster the cool to resume my reading. So, although I wasn't much interested in nature, I stared out of the window, and saw advertising hoardings, guard-huts, ramps and telegraph poles. At the end of a quarter hour the lady found some change, handed it to me, said thank you, and joined me in looking out of the window. I took up my newspaper and read. The beautiful lady stood up, stretched, reached for the luggage rack, was unable to reach her suitcase, and stood there piteously. I felt compelled to get up, take down the surprisingly heavy suitcase, pretending that its weight was negligible, my muscles were bands of iron and steel, and the suitcase a down feather. I had to keep the blood from rushing into my face, discreetly mop the sweat that beaded on my brow, and with an elegant bow, say, "Madam!" I managed this feat, the lady opened her suitcase, a little gasp of perfume, soap and powder escaped from it, pulled out three books, and was evidently hunting for a fourth. All the while I sat there strickenly pretending to read, but actually wondering how I would ever get the suitcase back up on the luggage rack. Because there could be no doubt that I was condemned to return it to its resting place. Condemned to pick up an item that weighed more than I did, with effortless ease, and return it without turning purple. I silently tensed my muscles, loaded up with energy, and told my heart to be calm. The lady found her fourth book, shut the suitcase and made an attempt to lift it.

Her effort incensed me. Why did she pretend not to know that I was bound to relieve her of the task? Why not ask me directly for help, as required by morality and very nearly the law? What was she doing with such a heavy suitcase anyway? And seeing as she was, why hadn't she packed her reading matter separately? Why did she have to read, seeing as she would certainly enjoy herself more talking to me right away, instead of allowing an hour to pass for the sake of decency? Why was she so beautiful that her helplessness was multiplied tenfold? And why was she a lady, and not a gentleman, a boxer, a sportsman, who might have picked up the suitcase with superb ease? My indignation was unavailing, I had to get up, say my "Allow me!" and with a superhuman effort hoist the suitcase up in the air. I stood on the seat, the suitcase was shaking in my hands—what if it should fall and crush the beautiful lady? It would have been unfortunate, but I don't think I would have felt any guilt. Finally, the suitcase lay up on the rack, and I flopped back into my seat.

The lady thanked me and opened a book. From that moment on, I pondered how best to leave compartment and lady. I wholeheartedly envied any man with the good fortune of travelling with such a beautiful woman. But seeing as it was me, I did not envy myself. With honest alarm, I speculated about further useful objects the suitcase was bound to be harbouring. I no longer had eyes for my newspaper. The scenery had my contempt. Just as well a gentleman entered the compartment, a young, bold, athletic-seeming gentleman, and much dimmer than me. The lady set down her book. After a quarter hour, the gentleman made an idiotic remark, and the beautiful woman tinkled. He had presence of mind, quick-wittedness, he was capable of being entertaining, and surely of lifting a suitcase as well. He had no apprehensions, he would surely vanquish me and win the heart of the beautiful lady. I on the other hand had my peace of mind back, watched with indifference as the suitcase went up and down, my heart no longer pounded, and I followed with deep enjoyment the movements of the beautiful lady and the unfolding of the adventure. I was happy to have pleasant companions who were irked by my presence and wished me to the devil. For turbid natures like mine there is no better society.

Frankfurter Zeitung, 19 September 1926

57

Morning at the Junction
(1927)

High summer. The train stops, and we hear the indefatiga-ble chirping of crickets in the fields, and the song of telegraph wires, which sounds like the whooshing of dark, eerie, otherworldly scythes. The railway junction lies at the confluence of mountains, fields, larks and sky. We get there at four in the morn-ing, no sooner and no later. The thoughtful timetable has arranged for the June sun and the passenger to reach the junction at the same time.

The porters are already up, so we aren't on our own. Rails run off in every direction, elastic as stretched rubber bands, tightly held by far-off stations to keep them from snapping back to the junction. The station has a cosy restaurant in first, second and third class. Hospitable as it is, it accommodates a red vending machine with gold writing, six apertures for coins, a curly-wurly handle and a baroque gable that looks like a nod to some miniature gatehouse. All the stations I ever saw in my childhood had vending machines like that. I associate their aspect with the mysterious sound of the signals, the sound of the golden spoon in the glass that experts can interpret, but which to the layman says only that a train is coming from who knows where. Throughout my childhood, I saw those red vending machines. If I were to throw in a coin now, I could pull out the chocolate I would have wanted twenty years ago that I no longer care for.

The small green news-stand is still closed, as it's thought to be too early for tobacco. The restaurant however is already giving out coffee, in freshly rinsed glasses, that a girl lifts out of their bath and holds up against the sun. Yesterday's newspapers are on sale, not knowing that they are yesterday's. But the sense of today is so strong that the newspapers look very old. The sunrise alone is enough to refute their news.

If you leave the station, you will see a hamlet so small that you wonder why the junction is here of all places, and if it is here, by blind chance, then why it hasn't grown into a city; and how it can be the aim of a place to remain a junction and concentrate its whole significance outside itself, in the railway station; and how this place, even though every morning a train stops and passengers alight, is so deeply asleep it doesn't even seem to know it is a junction at all. Only the cocks in all innocence are crowing. Not until five o'clock does a man with a rake and a watering can potter down the single street to his allotment. The barber is still asleep behind the fence that has his gleaming bronze basin affixed to it, a mirror in the sun. No. 76 is where the fire brigade's trumpeter lives, there is a sign that says as much. His ground floor window is open, he gets up, kisses his wife, pulls a shirt on, and goes out to perform his ablutions. I stand outside his window in the hope that he will play me something, even though there's no fire. An intellectual summer visitor is awake already. He is just setting off, swinging his cane, traces of soft boiled egg about his lips, up a mountain, the newspaper in his pocket, a subscriber to the bitter end, the highest peak.

How time creeps, when observed like this through a magnifying glass! Another three hours—and the clock on the church tower is slow. A stream drives a mill, a shepherd his sheep, a wind the morning fog. The news-stand at the station is still closed. It has glass walls, like someone sleeping with their eyes open. The girl at the buffet is still rinsing glasses. She has a plait, an apron, and her mouth is a little red splotch. Were you out for a walk? her mouth asks, while her hands rinse glasses. Are you travelling far?

Yes. — Will you take me with you then? — And because I fail to say yes (the junction makes one so slow on the uptake!), I answer her question with another: Would you like to come with me then?

Oh yes, she says.

Probably she asks the question every morning, aloud or to herself, to some man who's waiting for the train, travelling far away, and hence likeable. I should like to be old now, to cover my cowardice. If I had a white beard, or was at least bald, then I could say to her: Stay here in the junction, miss! It's sometimes better to watch men leave, than be whisked away by them. Because if you're old, you're allowed to comfort girls—and yourself as well—with sage lies.

I don't take her with me, but I do take her hand. She wipes it on her apron—the movement is expressive of her resignation. She has wiped out her desires, with a sponge. Bon voyage! she says. I'm looking at the rails, I don't look her in the eye, otherwise we would have had to kiss—which we're afraid to do, because we're stupid, scared and practical-minded.

Frankfurter Zeitung, 24 June 1927

Part VIII

Ending

The Old Poet Dies
(1927)

A few days ago in the *Frankfurter Zeitung* I wrote a piece about the eighty-year-old Linz poet Eduard Samhaber. I concluded with the wish that the eighty-year-old might live to be a hundred. Now I read in the *Kölnische Volkszeitung* that three days before the appearance of my piece, and as I can now relate, on the very day I was writing it, Eduard Samhaber passed away. I wrote it at night. Samhaber, the dead man, was dear to me, and I didn't know while I was wishing him a long life that I was actually writing his funeral oration. On the day of his death, moreover, he was given an honour: the silver medal that the Austrian republic gives its distinguished poets. Now both the state medal and my wishes are redundant. Genuine violets will sprout from his bones—and he will have eternal life in the section of paradise that is reserved for poets. He has put aside his wonderful earthly face and left it to us to remember him by. Honour to his beautiful inheritance!

Frankfurter Zeitung, 2 April 1927

The Third Reich, a Dependency of Hell on Earth

(1934)

After seventeen months, we are now used to the fact that in Germany more blood is spilled than the newspapers use printers' ink to report on it. Probably Goebbels, the overlord of German printers' ink, has more dead bodies on the conscience he doesn't have, than he has journalists to do his bidding, which is to silence the great number of these deaths. For we know now that the task of the German press is not to publicize events but to silence them; not only to spread lies but also to suggest them; not just to mislead world opinion—the pathetic remnant of the world that still has an opinion—but also to impose false news on it with a baffling naïveté. Not since this earth first had blood spilled on it has there been a murderer who has washed his bloodstained hands in as much printers' ink. Not since lies were first told in this world has a liar had so many powerful loudspeakers at his disposal. Not since betrayal was first perpetrated in this world was a traitor betrayed by another, greater traitor: has there been such a contest between traitors. And, alas, never has the part of the world that has not yet sunk into the night of dictatorships been so dazzled by the hellish glow of lies, or so deafened and dulled by the screaming of so many lies. For hundreds of years, we have been accustomed to lies going around on tiptoe. The epoch-making discovery of modern dictatorships is the invention of the loud lie, based on the psychologically correct assumption that people will believe a shout when they doubt speech. Since the onset of the Third Reich the lie, in spite of the saying, has walked on long legs.* It no longer follows on the heels of the truth, it races on ahead of it. If Goebbels is to be credited with a stroke of genius, then surely it is this: he has caused official truth to walk with the limp he has himself. The officially sanctioned German truth has been given its own club foot. It is no fluke but a knowing joke on the part of history that the first German minister of propaganda has a limp.

But this sophisticated attention to detail on the part of world history has had little effect on foreign reporters. It would be wrong to suppose that journalists from England, America, France, etc. didn't fall for the lying loudspeakers and loud speakers of Germany. Journalists too are children of their time. It is a mistake to think that the world has an accurate sense of Germany. The reporter who has sworn to be true to the facts bows to the *fait accompli* as before an idol, the *fait accompli* that is recognized by powerful politicians, rulers and wise men, philosophers, professors and artists. Even ten years ago a murder, never mind where and of whom, would have been a thing of horror to the world. Since the time of Cain innocent blood that cried out to heaven has found hearing on earth. Even the murder of Matteotti—not so long ago!—stirred the living to dread. But ever since Germany has started using its loudspeakers to drown out the cries of blood, these have only been heard in heaven, on earth they have been degraded to a common news item. Schleicher and his young wife were murdered. Ernst Röhm and many others have been murdered. Many of them were murderers themselves. But it wasn't a just, but an unjust punishment that befell them. Cleverer, nimbler murderers have murdered others, less

* Long legs: German says *Lügen haben kurze Beine*—Lies have short legs.

clever, less nimble than themselves. In the Third Reich, it isn't just Cain killing Abel; it's also a super Cain killing plain Cain. It is the only country in the world where there aren't just murderers but murderers raised to the power of n.

And as I say, the spilt blood cries out to that heaven where the terrestrial reporters do not sit. They sit instead at Goebbels's press conferences. They are only human. Stunned by loudspeakers, baffled by the speed with which suddenly, in spite of every natural law, limping truths start to sprint, and the short legs of lies stretch out to overtake the truth, these reporters tell the world only what they are told in Germany, and hardly anything of what is happening in Germany.

No reporter is equal to a country where, for the first time since the creation of the world, not just physical but metaphysical anomalies are propagated: monstrous hell births; cripples that run; arsonists who incinerate themselves; fratricidal brothers; devils biting themselves in the tail. It is the seventh circle of hell whose dependency on earth is known as "The Third Reich".

Pariser Tageblatt, 6 July 1934

60

Far from the Native Turf
(1934)

I

Heinrich Heine is a poet for the ages and a perennially current writer. His lasting, so to speak, continually reawakening journalistic relevance vies with his poetic immortality. He was always a darling of the Graces and of women, and therefore always detested by Germany. This country that is forever trying to prove itself was minutely understood, loved, pitied and despised by him. He is its prophet. He foresaw the course Germany would take. Read him, and save yourself the daily reports of events in Germany. Every new German calamity bears him out. Every new pubescent phase of this people that is unable to attain maturity and as a result sees itself (and unfortunately other countries as well) as "dynamic", confirms Heinrich Heine's words about his fatherland. No wonder the number of Heine biographies almost matches the number of German catastrophes. The newest one, to our knowledge, is by Antonina Vallentin, published in French by Gallimard.

Probably it is the discreetest of all the Heine biographies, cautious, tender, forgiving, and more than half in love. The personal wretchedness of the poet, the happiness and grief of his love affairs are discerned with greater reliability than literary science and research can establish for a fact. Which is not to say that this book lacks knowledge. On the contrary: it is full of diligence. But it takes the gentle hand and sensitive heart of a woman to order so much knowledge that it appears only in the background. It sometimes seems as though the author had known Heine personally, and only then, as if to cross-check her impressions, consulted the more substantial and objective sources. And all the time, the epoch that Heine crowned and represented is not lost from sight, nor his continuing relevance, which we noted above. A very alert publicistic sense compels the tender eye of the authoress, watching the suffering darling of the Muses with pity, to keep returning to the actual scene, and to draw the analogy between those days and ours.

It is a distinguished book. The author walks in the shadow of her great hero—and yet her discretion betrays her sympathetic presence. The book, written in German, appears in French, one of the few worthy gifts that German writers across the borders of German barbarism have been able to offer the French admirers of Heine and his spirit.

II

AN EVIDENTLY SIGNIFICANT coincidence brings us, almost simultaneously, a new book by the noted Heine biographer and politician Hermann Wendel. Readers who are acquainted with pre- and post-1914 politics will need no introduction to Hermann Wendel. Born in Metz of German parents, tending in his heart a love of France and a wish for a free and dignified Germany, Hermann Wendel was a socialist MP out of poetic élan, an active politician from idealism, not a realist but an idealist politician, if you like. The very embodiment of the frontier man, German and Gaul, European in a way that no longer exists.

Hermann Wendel has now published his memoirs (*Recollections of a Citizen of Metz*) with the Strasbourg house of Mésange: written in German, felt in European, like everything from the pen of this politician, historian and publicist. These memoirs radiate a kindly melancholy, a forgiving melancholy. (Wendel certainly has much to forgive socialism and Germany.) His book is important, and of broad interest, even though seeming to contain only personal experience. But Wendel has the grace of the writer and the man of the world. Everything he says is cultured, delicate, powerful, valid and rich in suggestion.

III

THE THIRD BOOK that seems to me worthy of being mentioned in the same breath as the two foregoing are the thoughts of the well-known Berlin lawyer Dr. Alfred Apfel on the background of German justice (*Les dessous de la justice Allemande*, again from Gallimard.) These are revelations. Germans reading this book will recall with pain that Germany was all set to become a Third Reich long before Hitler was ever thought of. French readers will see what they were slow to learn, and perhaps have learned too late. (By their justice ye shall know them!) Apfel, himself imprisoned by the Hitler regime, has managed to escape to France, and it seems to me both indicative and correct that these revelations first appear in French. If one has escaped to France, then how else thank this country except by illuminating the French. It's not just a thank you, it's also meritorious, whatever our barbarians may say about "high treason". Remember, our fatherland is not the one where we fare well! A country where bad things happen and more bad things are prepared than in any Hell's kitchen, no longer deserves to be called a fatherland. We can't love soil that puts forth such weeds.

Each chapter of Alfred Apfel's book has an epigraph from Heinrich Heine, that prophetic and forever momentous Heinrich Heine whom Antonina Vallentin has illuminated.

Pariser Tageblatt, 14 July 1934

61

Grillparzer:* A Portrait
(1937)

I

Peevish, cantankerous, grumpy, he concealed his shyness behind an aggressive humility, a modesty that was in point of fact haughtiness. He was no "sweet-natured Austrian", more the opposite: a highly awkward, even gloomy one. It was as though, in consequence of his promise to be a classical representative of the monarchy, he felt primarily the need to go against the picture-postcard notions the other German peoples had of Austria (and this before the advent of the picture postcard). At the same time he went against the popular type of the prickly loyal subject that was so popular in the upper echelons of his own country. He never revolted, because he was in permanent rebellion. He rebelled out of conservatism, as a supporter of hierarchical order and a defender of traditional values, which he saw as under attack, neglected, offended against not from below, but from above. Devoted to the House of Habsburg and the pan-German and transnational ideas that it symbolized, he still viewed the Emperor with a degree of cool and irritation; embittered too by his experience, which had proved to

* Franz Seraphicus Grillparzer (1791–1872), Austrian dramatist and moralist.

him that those in power had no vocation for it, he set himself, a poor, weak, capriciously treated official, a playwright exposed to the favour, disfavour and indifference of others, to defend the inheritance, the great, misunderstood inheritance of the Roman Emperor. Yes, he enjoyed "the very highest approbation", he sought and required it as a formal affirmation of his idealizing picture—not sloppily idealizing, more reconstructive—but this recognition was a cold sun. And he felt such a chill already! He was full of suspicion. His great, pale eyes seemed to have been made to listen as much as look, they were hearkening lights. They made enemies for him, and awakened further mistrust. In Austria, people with listening eyes were not popular. (Only Beethoven was an exception: he was deaf.)

Rarely was he seized by yearning to be away, the longing to leave the limits of his extensive, varied fatherland that could be home and abroad at one and the same time. Once, he set off to pay a visit to Goethe. Cultured readers will know the lamentable outcome of this encounter between the humble man who hid behind his modesty, and the great one who used his greatness to keep the world at arm's length. It was the Kahlenberg's encounter with Olympus: tragic, because it led to the underestimation of the Kahlenberg.* Grillparzer had hoped for a while to escape the peevishness of his constricting homeland, and to be allowed to breathe the atmosphere of global horizons for two days, no more than two wretched days. And he returned home more shaken than broken, more sad than disappointed, enriched by the experience that his Catholic faith affirmed: that no man can become a demigod and that even a genius is limited to the standard five senses, a few crumbs of intuition, and sometimes a degree of good fortune that is nothing compared to the grace of suffering.

He filed this experience away with the others. He actively provoked the disfavour of fate. Perhaps the reason he went to

* Kahlenberg: a hill outside Vienna, affording celebrated views of the city.

Goethe was to see with his own eyes the happiness of a fortunate man, his better and his opposite. It was like a Friday going out to see what a Sunday is like, and then going home, satisfied and sad that he was Friday.

II

LOVE ENTAILS RISK. One has a justifiable dread of risks. They are distantly related to revolts, uprisings and civil disturbances. The object of love is not responsible for the unpredictable character of the feeling that is called a "passion"—and passion of course in the original sense of "suffering". For all this the object of love, the individual woman, is of course not responsible, but as a type, as "woman", she represents unpredictability, danger, the potential for revolution and sin. In a world of few certainties, she makes commotion and drama more probable. She can splinter the steps of hierarchic order, in the way that a child might take it into its head to loosen and break the rungs of a ladder. Grillparzer is happily in love. He fears only the other sex. Bizarre descendant from Austrian troubadours, he turns the saying of the Minnesingers on its head and loves *before* he adores: a moralist, not a courtier—no more than he is a courtier in his attitude to the Emperor. He wasn't a flatterer, he was silent: his silence was reproachful.

The way he was, and the way he portrayed himself, he should have demanded to be loved: not just as a man of sorrows, but as a grump, uncomfortable and pedantic, knowing that such qualities are antipathetic to a woman's heart. There was arrogance in him, uncertainty and the pleasure of self-denial. He fulfilled, nourished, fed his desire by denying it.

So he didn't "know" woman in the Biblical sense. Nor did he find friends among men either. Love nuzzled him, trustfully, with interest. He could have reached out to stroke it, but instead he pushed it away; like a traveller in the desert who persists in taking an oasis for a mirage, and in his mind pushed it back to the unattainable blue horizon. He didn't trample on happiness where it offered itself to him, but he did push it away with both hands, declined it, avoided it, looked the other way.

III

HE HAD THE GIFT of intuition, and he dived into the future like others into the past. None of his professionally clairvoyant political contemporaries could see the future as well as he, who wrote: "From humanity through nationality to bestiality". Not a *bon mot*, but a cry of fear in view of the looming disintegration of the monarchy, the final victory of awakening national barbarism. A cry of fear, palpable even in his victory cry to Radetzky: "All Austria is in your camp!" Actually, the hinterland was by no means still intact, the army alone represented it. Sadová* cast an enormous shadow. Austria triumphed at sea, against the Italians, at Lissa,† not in the north, on land, against Germany. Not only the Austrian army, but the idea of the cosmopolitan German was smashed by his stepbrother, the nationalist German, whose watchwords were: centralize, vanquish, oppress, rule—the opposite of the unfairly taken against Latin motto (because misunderstood and misapplied for domestic politics): *Divide et impera!* A subtle translation would be: decentralize and exercise influence! Not: divide and rule!

But how many—even then—had a proper understanding of Latin? Since Joseph II, aping Prussian centralism and enlightenment à la Frederick the Great, reined in the church and—surely without meaning to or knowing he was doing it—laid the moral and intellectual basis for the subsequent nationalist arrogance of German Austrians vis-à-vis the other Austrians (the "dictatorship"

* Sadová, or Königgrätz: the decisive battle in 1866 of the Austro–Prussian War.
† Lissa: sea-battle in the Adriatic in the same war.

one might call it), one of the last refuges of universal Latinity was taken away, destroyed from above, even though the Catholic Emperor of course had none of the Protestant and Voltairean élan (the dynamism, as we say today) of Prussia. Grillparzer perhaps marks the beginning of the (political) *Weltschmerz* of the Austrian writer. At least, it was Grillparzer who gave it its classic expression: the anguish that understands that the Europe of the Middle Ages, Latin, universalist, suspending national differences—which in Austria still had force and being—was bound to be followed by the Europe of the Reformation and the French Revolution, the Europe of Napoleon and Bismarck. "From humanity through nationality to bestiality" means: from Erasmus through Luther, Frederick II, Napoleon, Bismarck, to the clutch of dictators we have today.

There were in those days few representatives of this (Catholic, political) *Weltschmerz*: liberalism was just beginning to convert the virtues of Austria into a stage set, lightness into flippancy; the actual "*heuriger*"* is tart, but the poems and songs squeezed from it make a saccharine lemonade. An acute conservative ear could discern the worldwide victory of the waltz and its offspring, the operettas of Lehár. From that "Grace" that takes its name from Greek antiquity and the Catholic *gratia*, was derived the export article: "Austrian cheer"; from etiquette, the stern daughter of Spain, any amount of bending-and-scraping compliancy. Can you blame Grillparzer!? He was surrounded by so much applause that he could only assert himself in lament. Empty laughter hurt him, privately as well as publicly. A minor transgression, the wrong word, even a clumsy gesture was enough to antagonize him. He reacted with extreme sensitivity—the most vengeful of all human weaknesses—with sometimes wounding arrogance (though never crossing the boundary into vulgarity). Such episodes only made him sadder. He suffered a hangover after wrath as others did after excess.

* Newly made white wine, drunk and celebrated in the hills around Vienna.

IV

SPAIN IS AUSTRIA'S NEIGHBOUR in history. The Counter-Reformation is a distant, calmer cousin to the Inquisition. The Habsburgs are Spaniards who took on the Austrian character and kept their Spanish ceremonials. These ceremonials, rigorous and assimilating at once, stand up to the rising tide of frivolity in Austria. The flag pairs black with yellow. The black watches over the yellow. The double eagle, golden, over both halves, watches over unity. Spain is Austria's neighbour in history, and Grillparzer's in literature.

He is the only German classic author of Spanish antecedents. Like the Habsburgs, he comes from Spain. He is Calderon's descendant. It's not just the form of the *Ahnfrau.** It's not the metre at all, more the cadence. It's the attempt to couple the nervous clicking of the castanets with the steady iambs of German. A vain attempt, by the way. The *Ahnfrau* remains a classic oddity, mainstay of the Viennese Burgtheater and the school syllabus, but requiring the sanction of the k. and k. Ministry of Education and Culture.

Grillparzer subsequently gave up metre and rhythm, but not the melody of Spain. It flowed quite naturally into the native speech of Vienna. The *grandezza* of Spanish ceremonial was just as easily joined to the lightness of Austria. (If the percussion that opens the Radetzky March fails to remind you of castanets, then you have no ear for music.)

The melancholy of the narrative prose is not the golden *Wehmut*—the expression of Austrian sadness—but an expression of sternness. Picture a pleasant landscape in a black frame. The aphoristic prose is not satirical or campaigning as Grillparzer's prose is, but furious. It is the aphoristic expression of a judge, a public prosecutor; or say it, an inquisitor, who is laying into his own people; sometimes with the resources of a card-carrying prophet.

* *Die Ahnfrau (The Ancestress)*, Grillparzer's play of 1817.

Never does bitterness turn into jeering. Never does a jibe become a pleasantry. Strict obedience to literary genre. Here too, here above all, the laws of the hierarchy. There is a Spanish anger when Grillparzer scolds. Austria knows no rage, it dwindles into a ticking-off: even rage finds its own tradesmen's entrance.

Grillparzer's anger was the expression of a subtle implacability softened by Latin Austria, and then amended by Spanish. His indignation was limited, personal, not meant as incitement or contagion, on the contrary: a rebellion of high-mindedness within the boundaries of the individual. He was the classic instance of a rebel who is at the same time a true reactionary: a phenomenon which the recent fashion of labelling everything rebellious and indignant, everything consciously eccentric and apart, as "revolutionary" is incapable of understanding. When Grillparzer stands in opposition to the Emperor, he does so by being more imperial than the Emperor. He mutinies against the relaxing of the ceremonial from above. He watches over the supposed guardians of the hierarchy. He is, if you will allow the expression, a reactionary par excellence, an individual anarchist reactionary. A posterity impertinently, dictatorially occupying the past is pleased to claim Grillparzer as a victim of reactionary Austria, as if he was one of the helpless, common or garden victims of reaction. When all the time he was a rebel out of reaction, of free will. His anger against the rulers came—in today's parlance—not from the left, but the right. He was as Spanish as the Habsburgs, and as Roman as the Pope: the only conservative revolutionary in the history of Austria.

V

SUCCESSES TASTED BITTER to him, almost like failures. Of course, Austria had its connived-at failures, its failures *in spe*, a sort of parallel to pre-censorship. Displeasure at court, not even spontaneous displeasure, but a factitious displeasure bred by snoops and tell-tales, fed by intrigue, slander, malice, could hinder even a failure, and took from the writer the possibility of hearing the voice of an audience. To be taken off the programme, to be scorned, rejected, whistled at by an audience, all that spells an honest, so to speak, earned failure. But to "meet with disfavour" before the writer is even allowed to throw down his challenge, to suffer a fate that is itself a challenge and that is too powerful for you to measure yourself against, is a difficult lot, an Austrian curse. It's like being imprisoned without charge. Under these conditions success, honour even, could not bring satisfaction, much less pleasure. And so success and failure tasted equally bitter to him. It was even possible that success brought pain, and failure only a long-awaited, almost yearned-for melancholy. One may feel at home in misery, gradually begin to love it like a dear friend. There is a condition in which one fears joyful surprises, Christmas at the wrong time, presents that are like assaults, and at the sight of which one is even forced to smile. Success can be a torment.

He saw through hope, came to like doubt, but didn't lose his faith. It's not possible to lose faith: after all, it's faith in God. Scepticism doesn't hurt such faith: on the contrary, it accompanies it, sometimes even supports it. The unreliability of the world is a consequence of its inadequacy. You don't oppose its pressure, its mood, its despotism, by open revolt, which can have no other outcome than catastrophic inadequacy, in other words: disorder, the greatest of all dangers to a human, but by a retreat into the depth, into the cave of the self. An association, impossible to dismiss, with the image of the gloomy Spanish monarch burying himself alive.* He doesn't live off to the side, but in the depths. From below he sees more accurately, with a juster bitterness and a moral bitterness, the facility, the poverty of the high-ups, and more clearly the

---

* Burying himself alive: Charles V, the Holy Roman Emperor, (1500–1558), who retired to the monastery of St. Yuste where he died.

summit of heaven; by day the stars that populate it (even by day). The dead on all sides are nearer to him than the living can be above him. He hears their breathing, the silent sleep of the time-conquerors. They have conquered this era that is so antagonistic and so wrong. It is made up of darkness and a false dawn, hailed by clueless, optimistic, noble, revolutionary bowler hats, feared by bitter men of our sort, who are not colour blind and understand exactly how much human blood is needed to brew that "dawn's fiery glow". It is soaked full of the blood of the great revolution, of the wars of Napoleon, when for the first time the cry rang out: "Nations, awaken!" The response of our dour species is: "From humanity through nationality to bestiality."

Oh, those times! The hierarchical institutions are still intact, but the men in charge of them are slothful, thoughtless, unprincipled. They embody the randomness and disorder they have been called in to oppose. They are not called, they are hired. They have the perplexing ability—the curse, more—of oppressing and retreating at one and the same time. The astringency of the ancestors and forefathers, put to the service of an implacable idea, is as different from the facile, illegitimate desire to press, the tyranny of the ruler, as dark is from black. Anarchy wears the mask of legitimacy. Meanwhile, a second anarchy, following on the heels of the first, makes ready to fight it. Lonely and timorous on the surface, protected in the depths. Charles V went to the grave alive; he felt the end was nigh, he too had no confederates.

VI

THE END OF THE GREAT but perceptibly shrinking empire still has one noble aspect, for all its inner cracks, flaws, pettinesses and rottennesses. A noble death. The victorious troops have something of the classic élan of Lipizzaner greys, the courtliest beasts in Europe, who have the symbolic nobility of heraldic animals.

Austrian troops go to battle in snow-white tunics. Their victories are the classic successes of an outlived tradition. Their defeats carry symbolic weight. It's the last hurrah of the old knightliness, losing out to plebeian technology; the unprotected advance of massed ranks against small, mobile, camouflaged units in broken field; the highly visible snow white, a noble target, against a blue that was invisible in fog (and called "Prussian blue" ever since); the cavalry charge against fortified artillery positions. It's the end of feudalism: dying in the old armour, fighting a parvenu who is about to put on the false crown, a legal figment of an emperor. Seen from a higher angle, the Junker becomes an ignorant beneficiary of the great Revolution and the only genial *arriviste* of history: Napoleon.

Such is the catastrophe billowing around Grillparzer. His contemporaries—even the most significant of them—are not able to stand up to it. They are too small for such a comprehensive defeat, which confirms the decline of Charles V, and anticipates that of Karl in 1918. They take refuge in the treasury of home, in Austria, which is still capacious and various enough and has enough breath, but is now only "folklore" not "world". Its orientation has changed, too: now it is Zagreb, Sarajevo, Belgrade, Tehran, Constantinople; no more towards Ghent, Bruges, Antwerp, Amsterdam, Cologne, Frankfurt, Milan, Rome, Hanover—and the fraternal enemy Berlin. The great and important in Austria acquire the peripheral character of specialities—dialect dyes them all, even the cosmopolitan Viennese, not just the provincial "folk poets" and "local characters". Only Grillparzer kept the world in view, because he was the only one who suffered the pain of the lost, great, dry world. But Calderon and the Spanish antecedents of the Habsburgs became ever more remote, that is: his moral and intellectual origins are still less present than his material home, Switzerland. Twenty years ago the past was still there, instinct with life. Now it's shrouded in dimness and fog. Grillparzer alone remains, a monument, buried alive, a living monument, already crumbling. His face is like weathered stone, yellow-hued, as though there was something like stone parchment. His body, too, lean, knotty and stooped, is reminiscent of wood, root, rock. His statue is less stony than he is. His heart shines in his large eyes, loyal grey mirrors to a sunken world, large, bright lights that listened to the future, and picked up the terror of the final end. When he shut them for ever, not prematurely, not at the right moment, if anything too late, because death can sometimes be as cruel as life—Charon delayed—people only knew that a "classic", one of the "greats", "a Burgtheater dramatist", an Austrian pendant to the Académie Française-member, a retired senior civil servant, had gone on. And one knows still less today than then about how widely spanned his life's arc was, all the way from Alcázar to Königgrätz; from *grandezza* and ceremonial to vulgarity and the Prussians; from the Habsburgs to the Hohenzollerns: from humanity through nationality to bestiality.

Austria has no Pantheon, only its cemeteries and a Kapuzinergruft, and rightly so. They are all under the sward: Beethoven, Bruckner, Stifter, Raimund, Nestroy, Grillparzer. To represent Austria means to be misunderstood and maltreated in your lifetime; unappreciated after your death; and periodically, by the agency of anniversary celebrations, to be returned to obscurity.

Das Neue Tage-Buch (Paris), 4 December 1937

62

The Bitter Bread

(1939)

Day breaks, and the poor man wishes he could prolong the
night. It is December, admittedly, so the day begins late,
but it is still too early for him. Mornings are bad, but with the passage of time the poor man has learned that they need to be
withstood, because the day is waiting. Not all days are as bad as
their advance guard, the morning. Some, a rare few, have been surprisingly favourable, others, most, have been decidedly bad. But
you can't judge the day from the morning.

It is a tiny fourth-floor hotel room, with scarlet wallpaper, pat-
terned with yellow sunflowers. A nearby church clock strikes eight.
There is a rushing in the pipes, because a tenant on the first or
second floor is running a bath. Now the poor man taxes the running water himself. For two weeks the same towel has been
hanging over the brass rail. The towel is soiled by the dirt of the
past days, the bearable, the ordinary, and the decidedly bad days.
The bedding too is four weeks old. But in the morning you don't
absolutely have to look at it, and at night you can't see it, because
the overhead light fixture lights only the middle of the ceiling, it is
there mostly for the benefit of flies. The spiders lurk in dark corners, behind thick grey webs of their own making, probably waiting
for the poor man to switch off the light and feel his way, barefooted
from the door to bed. Then the flies will be trapped in the webs,

and will be rolled up, sucked dry and eaten. Because there is no creature that does not rob, steal, kill, eat and live. Only the poor man needs money, otherwise he cannot live.

That a poor man—of all things—needs money is no longer new. A poor man needs at least a small amount of money, it's the rich man who needs a lot. But it's easier for a rich man to get a lot of money than for a poor man to get a little; and it may be the same with spiders. The ones that are in advantageous corners with large densely woven nets will catch more flies. But even that is of little comfort to the poor man.

Least of all on Thursdays, and today is a Thursday. Because on this day the hotel presents its bill. If he had been able to pay a month in advance, then he wouldn't have to be in weekly dread of the landlord, and even Thursday might be bearable. As it is, though, it is very bad; and the worst aspect of it is the morning. And today, as already stated, is a Thursday.

Even so, the poor man washes, as he did on Tuesday and Wednesday before, and tries to find an unsoiled corner of the towel to dry himself on. But a towel has only four corners, and all are dirty. Not to speak of the middle.

His coat hangs on the doorknob, because the coat hook is so loosely anchored in the plaster that it can only manage to support his hat. The poor man puts his hat on, and only gets into his coat on the way down. He doesn't lock his room. He takes the key out, though, because he has to hand it in downstairs. He doesn't lock the room, out of rebellion against poverty, and as if someone on the stairs or anywhere would say to him: You really should be careful, you know. And as if he, the poor man, would get a chance to reply: There's no reason to. I've nothing to steal. But it doesn't occur to anyone to warn a poor man of thieves.

Everything the poor man has by way of possessions, he takes with him. It fits into a little suitcase, and one can't even claim that everything in the suitcase belongs to him: the pencils, the

shirt-patterns, the collar studs, the rolls of thread, the rayon stockings, the soaps, the flacons of perfume: everything is his "on
commission". First he has to sell the wares, hand over what they
fetch, and only then will he get a little money. The poor man
checks his wallet, where he keeps his notebook. That contains his
most important "recommendations", which is to say, names and
addresses of people who are rumoured to have more money than
a poor man, and at least enough for them to lock their rooms.
These people have been recommended to the poor man. But
people don't want to risk making themselves unpopular with their
friends. They think it will do less harm to the poor man if he makes
himself unpopular.

Without these "recommendations", one really wouldn't know
where to bend one's steps on leaving the hotel. As it is, one has at
least a direction, and it's probably better to go a little higher,
because hope lasts longer the higher up the recommendations live.
On the first floor, so thinks the poor man, he will encounter only
disappointment.

He sets himself to sell a dozen pencils. One wouldn't believe that
pencils fetch more than collar studs for instance, or how hard they
are to sell. If the poor man had ever been able to say he had sold a
dozen pencils, then he could say he had clinched a deal. As it is
though, selling only one pencil at a time, he tells himself he can rely
on retail customers. And he adds: nowadays. The times are bad, no
question. For rich people, perhaps. The poor man moves into their
area by saying: nowadays.

This Thursday though seems to want to herald a better phase.
One "recommendation" buys eighteen pencils and six shirt buttons
and tells the poor man not to come again for two months. Two
months is a very long time for a well-off person, licking his finger
and flipping the pages of his pocket calendar. That's all. But for a
poor man, two months are two eternities. If someone wanted him
to come back the day after tomorrow, even tomorrow, he wouldn't

be able to promise. You never know from where you'll be coming home at the end of a day. The poor man doesn't even know whether he'll be coming home at all. He walks into a bistro, drinks a cup of coffee, dunks a croissant. He doesn't quite give in to the pleasure of it, as he knows it's a Thursday.

But it's a good Thursday. Because before the onset of evening— and in December the days are so short, they're over almost before they've begun—the poor man has sold three pairs of ladies' stockings and has an order for three shirts (with attached collars). Who knows what he could sell, if only it wasn't Thursday, and also December 29th. Because on that day the poor man has to go round to the police. He has a document that has his name on it and where he comes from and where he lives. But what it doesn't say is how long he can stay there, and where he's allowed to go.

He is told nothing. He waits. Then he puts down his suitcase, and stands at a counter, and an official stamps his paper immediately; so quickly that the poor man is tempted to ask the official if he could use a couple of pencils. Luckily the poor man thinks twice about that, and he walks off. What else does he need? He can pay the rent. He can stay another fortnight. He can afford a sausage, a piece of cheese, a bottle of beer. The poor man is full of optimism. And on a Thursday.

He goes home, pays his bill, goes up to his room, and lies down in his bed. Today he doesn't even turn the light on: that's how contented the poor man is.

Parisier Tageszeitung, 3 January 1939

63

Furlough in Jablonovka
(1939)

The village of Jablonovka nestles in my memory like a jewel. Sometimes I am able to produce it, its thatched huts painted a pale blue wash, its one dwelling that was almost town-like because it had a shingle roof and a brown wooden door and two shallow steps leading up to it: just two. The white church with its tin dome stood on the little hill, in the middle of its fenced-in graveyard, a short way beyond the last of the dwellings—or a short way before the first of them, depending on where you were coming from. Left of the church gate was the bell tower, with its one big bell flanked by two junior bells. Behind the huts that stood on the twice-round village street, there was a slight incline, and a few of the huts seemed to be slowly scrambling up the hill. I was last in Jablonovka three months ago. It was 10 October, on a silvery morning that couldn't make up its mind whether to be warm or cold. Spots of thin mist lay over the stubble fields.

It was in the War. But Jablonovka, away from the main roads, had only been required to house an alternation of Austrian and Russian reserve troops and their general staffs. The women and children and the old men and the old priest had not come under any immediate threat for three years.

There were not many horses or vehicles, the animals looked ill-nourished, the geese and ducks as well, only the pigs looked respectable, but their numbers were down after many requisitions.

A few hours after we moved into Jablonovka we left it again. We have been through plenty of shelled villages. But this one— strange—was spared. If we stayed here, perhaps we would share in the miracle. Why not? Why shouldn't we stay here? Isn't a soldier worth as much as a duck, a soldier in the Twenty-First, or the Thirty-Fifth? You see—the village says—things can be peaceful too. Huts don't have to be on fire, shells don't have to go off. I don't mind if the odd aeroplane draws its circles. Then on Sundays my bells ring. Why not? High days and holy days can be celebrated. And—think about it—all those peasants born in me, grown up in me, they could have grown old, instead of dying. But I have plenty of peasant lads left. Sired by foreign soldiers maybe, but at least they did it here, in my fields and meadows, in my huts. I for one would like to continue to exist, with the help of God, away from the catastrophe.

Thus the village, but I wasn't able to listen to it for long. Until mid-December we were twenty miles east of there, on a quiet sector of the front. It was as though the village extended its benedictions to the trenches.

We were already receiving early Christmas parcels, and of course not opening them. I should say: I didn't receive any myself; I would certainly have opened them if I had, to be honest. I've always hated surprises. I neither wanted to give nor to get any. I was all alone amidst the expectant merriment of my comrades. Yes, our sector was quiet. But we had stood and continued to stand in the face of death. I was upset at the way men who had stared death in the face now collapsed into the tinsel and mawkishness that for the past hundred years or so had marked the birth of our Lord. To tell the truth, I was trembling at the thought of Christmas, or rather the things attending it. I fervently wished not to get any parcels from home—what was home anyway but a kind of glorified hinterland?—or consolatory surprises from my comrades. Nowhere had the manger at Bethlehem felt so near or the "parlour" with its "gifts" so far. "Christmas in the field" was something for war cor-respondents.

Then a miracle happened, not a postcard miracle, but a real one. We went into furlough on 19 December. We went to Jablonovka. You see, the village says, it can happen. It was deep in snow. Icicles dangled from the thatch over the tiny windows at the back. And when I wanted to look out onto the wintry street from the hut I'd been quartered in, I had to take a candle and melt a hole in the ice on the window. It closed up again in no time. The temperature was twenty below.

On Christmas Eve the peasants came into regimental HQ. They asked us for sixteen candles. Hanamak, our warrant officer, pro-duced eight, and cut them in half. Boys carved faces in hollow pumpkins, lit the candles inside them, and each of them had three pumpkins, and those were their Three Kings. Five boys, all sons of Frau Olszewska, had a manger they had carved themselves. It was a tiny hut, no more than fifteen inches high, painted green, three walls, an open stage. There were little bundles of actual hay inside. And if you poked your finger through a ring on the gable of the house, the whole thing seemed to rock by itself, and inside Mary was rocking her infant, the grey donkey shook its long grey ears, and the miniature Three Kings, who came out dressed in scarlet and gold, moved their trembly sleeves that were looped onto their wrists with thread. The star of Bethlehem shone within, as though it had come crashing through the thatch, and it turned out not to be a star at all, but a gold rosette as worn by our k. & k. officers. The war had reached Jablonovka after all.

The peasant woman I was billeted with was called Josefova Gargas, and I will never forget her. Although many of the village women had been widowed over the course of the war, she was the only one who was referred to as the Widow. Because her husband had died a natural death six months before the war began. She had three-year-old twins, a couple of winning bundles of flax. Her bony face enjoined her to silence and severity. But if you came to know her better, it was nothing but a doomed effort to suppress the kindness and goodness within her.

Karl Greiser, ensign, and pork-butcher in civilian life, slaughtered a pig. The widow scrubbed the floor, the table, the three chairs. When evening came, she set out a great dish with red stripes and blue flowers round the rim in the middle of the table. Two immense stoneware plates flanked it like children. Three wooden spoons, pale yellow as the table they lay on, looked like its children: they were wood of its wood. Kindling laid crosswise waited on the open hearth. And the heads of the twins smelled of that mustardy wartime soap: a smell of lye, dirty washing and poverty, especially poverty.

The mercury neither rose nor fell—and that was fine. A nothing sort of day disappeared into a clear night. Who could say how long we would remain here on furlough? Who could say where we would be dispatched to next? I dislike atmospherics. The field-post is carried out. Two parcels, all of two parcels. We are summoned to the officers' mess at eight, Rainacher and I. He dislikes atmospherics as well. We are both billeted with the widow Josefova. Because he has seniority, he sleeps in the bed, while I sleep on a straw mattress on the floor. We both excuse ourselves. We can't make the mess. We walk up the hill to midnight mass instead.

The sky glitters overhead, the snow glitters under our feet. It's as though the sky is a reflection of the snow. There's no point following the village street, which is all trampled. The snow was so seductive that it would have been a sin not to walk there, where it lay crisp and deep, noble, virginal, crystal and singing. So as not to encounter our comrades and to enjoy the night and the stars and the snow, we walked up the lane behind the houses. It was peaceful, no war anywhere. Ten or twelve times a searchlight crossed the sky, but even that seemed to be a kind of strolling, a peaceable pedestrian, paler than its brothers whom I knew better in the luminous sky.

The boys came in with their pumpkin lanterns. They sang. Stable and manger and donkey were nearby, if you could follow the singing. If you could believe them, the Saviour was born in Jablonovka, not far from Josefova Gargas's hut, and not two thousand years ago, but sixty at the most, and the oldsters still remembered the event. You could practically see the footprints of the Three Kings in the snow. The star was graspable. The Podolian plain was swaddled in faith, God was in Podolia, and Bethlehem was a hop and a skip away, much closer than the front.

Lights went out one after another, and the huts went dark. Only the sky and the snow were still gleaming as the village traipsed up the hill to the church. Its double doors were thrown open, and it was as though the altar was coming out to meet you, to welcome the visitors in its splendour. There were no pews. People stood and knelt. Although the doors were left open, it soon grew warm, it was as though the furs were warming me, and the candles, and the fervour and the Gloria after the Introitus: *Dominus dixit ad me: filius meus es tu, ego hodie genui te. Quare fremuerunt gentes; et populi meditate sunt inania?* What are the heathens purposing? What folly are the peoples pursuing? — *Et pastores erant in regione eadem vigilantes.* — And there were wakeful shepherds in that place—they were here next to us, next to Rainacher and me. We took the widow Josefova Gargas home between us. The door wasn't locked, no door in the village was ever locked, even though strange troops, Hungarians and Bosnians were furloughed here. There were wakeful shepherds here.

We sat down at the table, and ate our borsch with wooden spoons. Then we cut up the meat with our bayonets. We drank slivovitz from tea-glasses and canteens. My atheist friend Rainacher stretched comfortably on the chair, flung wide his arms and sang: *Gloria in excelsis deo.* He wasn't blaspheming. At three in the morning, we kissed the widow and the twins, gave them our four parcels, and went off to sleep. You take the bed tonight, Rainacher told me, I'll go on the floor. It's my present to you. And that's how it was. We were roused at six with marching orders.

Das Neue Tage-Buch (Paris), 23 September 1939

Coda

64

Cradle

(1931)

M y earliest memory goes back a very long way. It is separated from a subsequent almost uninterrupted chain of
memories commencing from my seventh year by a gap of several
years, so that this earliest experience seems to stand all alone, like
a brightly lit scene surrounded by darkness, and therefore all the
more luminous. It is a sad memory, or at any rate, one that made
me sad, for the first time in my life; and the scene, which, as I say,
has remained very close to me, still radiates a sort of groundless
melancholy, and therefore a true melancholy. The way a memory
can remain so distinctly preserved under a layer of forgetting
seems to heighten the importance of this early experience; there
is almost something symbolic about it. It was a clear winter's day.
I still seem to see, in the small room that was mine at the time, a
blue reflection of a cloudless sky, a thick, crystalline layer of snow
on the windowsill and a few intricate ice flowers on the right-hand
window. An old woman with a longish, grey brown shawl over her
head and shoulders enters the room. My mother takes the bedding
out of my cradle item by item, and lays it on a brown padded armchair. Then the woman in the shawl, who is not tall, steps up to my
cradle, says something, picks up the cradle with a surprising turn
of speed, holds it to her chest, as though it were a thing of no particular weight or dimensions, speaks for a long time, flashes her

long yellow teeth, and leaves our house. I am left feeling sad, inconsolably helpless and sad. I seem to understand that I have lost something irrecoverable. I have been in a certain sense robbed. I start to cry, and am taken to a large white bed, which is my mother's. There I fall asleep.

At this point the memory ends. The next four years are shrouded in shadow, in the thick shadow of forgetting. Later on, it transpires that my mother has no recollection of this day. Ten years later, she was unable to tell me when and to whom she had given my cradle. I wasn't surprised, nor was I upset with her. She had merely missed the first grief of my life. She had no idea. The thing that upsets me is that she no longer knew whether it was summer or winter. By chance I was able to establish later who took the cradle and when. I must have been three years old at the time. I have the feeling that on that day, in that hour I became a grown-up—only briefly perhaps, but long enough to be sad, as sad as a grown-up, and perhaps for a better reason.

Die Literarische Welt, 17 December 1931

Index

ABOUT THE AUTHOR

Joseph Roth was born Moses Joseph Roth to Jewish parents on September 2, 1894, in Brody in Galicia, in the extreme east of the then Habsburg Empire; he died on May 27, 1939, in Paris. He never saw his father—who disappeared before he was born and later died insane—but grew up with his mother and her relatives. After completing school in Brody, he matriculated at the University of Lemberg (variously Lvov or Lviv), before transferring to the University of Vienna in 1914. He served for a year or two with the Austro-Hungarian Army on the Eastern Front—though possibly only as an army journalist or censor. Later he was to write: "My strongest experience was the War and the destruction of my fatherland, the only one I ever had, the Dual Monarchy of Austria-Hungary."

In 1918 he returned to Vienna, where he began writing for left-wing papers, occasionally as "Red Roth", "*der rote Roth*". In 1920 he moved to Berlin, and in 1923 he began his distinguished association with the *Frankfurter Zeitung*. In the following years he travelled throughout Europe, filing copy for the *Frankfurter* from the south of France, the USSR, Albania, Germany, Poland, and Italy. He was one of the most distinguished and best-paid journalists of the period—being paid at the dream rate of one deutsche mark per line. Some of his pieces were collected under the title of one of them, *The Panopticum on Sunday* (1928), while some of his reportage from the Soviet Union went into *The Wandering Jews*. His gifts of style and perception could, on occasion, overwhelm his subjects, but he was a journalist of singular compassion. He observed and warned of the rising Nazi scene in Germany (Hitler actually appears by name in Roth's first novel, in 1923), and his 1926 visit to the USSR disabused him of most—but not quite all—of his sympathy for Communism.

When the Nazis took power in Germany in 1933, Roth immediately severed all his ties with the country. He lived in Paris—where he had been based for some years—but also in Amsterdam, Ostend, and the south of France, and wrote for émigré publications. His royalist politics were mainly a mask for his pessimism; his last article was called "Goethe's Oak at Buchenwald". His final years were difficult; he moved from hotel to hotel, drinking heavily, worried about money and the future. What precipitated his final collapse was hearing the news that the playwright Ernst Toller had hanged himself in New York. An invitation from the American PEN Club (the organization that had brought Thomas Mann and many others to the States) was found among Roth's papers. It is tantalizing but ultimately impossible to imagine him taking ship to the New World, and continuing to live and to write: his world was the old one, and he'd used it all up.

Roth's fiction came into being alongside his journalism, and in the same way: at café tables, at odd hours and all hours, peripatetically, chaotically, charmedly. His first novel, *The Spider's Web*, was published in instalments in 1923. There followed *Hotel Savoy* and *Rebellion* (both 1924), hard-hitting books about contemporary society and politics; then *Flight Without End*, *Zipper and His Father*, and *Right and Left* (all *Heimkehrerromane*—novels about soldiers returning home after the war). *Job* (1930) was his first book to draw considerably on his Jewish past in the East. *The Radetzky March* (1932) has the biggest scope of all his books and is commonly reckoned his masterpiece. There follow the books he wrote in exile, books with a stronger fabulist streak in them, full of melancholy beauty: *Tarabas*, *The Hundred Days*, *Confession of a Murderer*, *Weights and Measures*, *The Emperor's Tomb*, and *The Tale of the 1002nd Night*.

ABOUT THE TRANSLATOR

Michael Hofmann, the son of the German novelist Gert Hofmann, was born in 1957 in Freiburg. At the age of four he moved to England. He has published poems and reviews widely in England and in the United States, where he now teaches at the University of Florida in Gainesville.

He has edited the *Faber Book of Twentieth Century German Poems*; translated the selected poems of Durs Grünbein (*Ashes for Breakfast*, 2005), Günter Eich (*Angina Days*, 2010) and Gottfried Benn (*Impromptus*, 2014); and published two books of critical pieces, *Behind the Lines* and *Where Have You Been?*, as well as six books of poems, including a *Selected Poems* in 2008.

Michael Hofmann has translated some eighty works of German prose (from authors including Thomas Bernhard, Bertolt Brecht, Elias Canetti, Hans Fallada, Gert Hofmann, Ernst Jünger, Franz Kafka, Irmgard Keun, Wolfgang Koeppen, Herta Müller, Erich Maria Remarque, Peter Stamm, Wim Wenders and Markus Werner). The present volume is his fourteenth translation from Joseph Roth, whom he first translated in 1990; he won the PEN/ Book of the Month Club Prize for *The String of Pearls* in 1998, and the Helen and Kurt Wolff Translation Prize for *Rebellion* in 2000. For other translations he was awarded the IMPAC/ Dublin Literary Award, the Thornton Wilder Prize for Translation and the Oxford Weidenfeld Translation Prize (twice). He is a Foreign Member of the American Academy of Arts and Sciences, and of the Deutsche Akademie für Sprache und Dichtung.

Also available from Granta Books
www.grantabooks.com

WHAT I SAW

Reports from Berlin 1920–33

Joseph Roth

Translated and with an introduction
by Michael Hofmann

'These brilliant and quixotic pieces immortalize the everyday life of
1920s Berlin ... An instant classic' Roy Foster, *Financial Times*

'A supreme observer, a cynical romantic with a flair for prophecy
and an understanding of the slow fester of moral outrage ...
Outstanding' Eileen Battersby, *Irish Times*

'His slivers of Berlin life during the Weimar Republic
catch a city juddering with a sense of its own modernity,
even as he listens for sighs escaping through the cracks.
Tender, caustic [and] thrilling' David Jays, *Observer*

'Marvellous ... proof that [Roth] is as brilliant and original a
journalist as he is a storyteller, casting his eye and cocking his
ear where lesser writers never venture' *Sunday Times*

'Nonstop brilliance, irresistible charm and continuing
relevance ... A book that gives so much delight without
resorting to fraudulent means or shoddy thinking. The hardest
thing about writing this review is that I want to quote every
sentence' Jeffrey Eugenides, *New York Times*